$\mathcal{M}$ UNITED ETHODISTS and the Sacraments

Gayle C. **FELTON**

ABINGDON PRESS/Nashville

UNITED METHODISTS AND THE SACRAMENTS

Copyright © 2007 by Abingdon Press

This book is printed on acid-free paper.

Unless otherwise indicated, Scripture quotations in this publication are from the *Holy Bible: New Revised Standard Version*, copyright © 1989 by the Division of Christian Education of the National Council of the Churches of Christ in the United States of America, and are used by permission. All rights reserved.

Library of Congress Cataloging-in-Publication Data

ISBN-13 978-0-687-49215-2

MANUFACTURED IN THE UNITED STATES OF AMERICA

07 08 09 10 11 12 13 14 15 16—10 9 8 7 6 5 4 3 2 1

Contents

Introduction

I HAVE BEEN PREPARING TO WRITE THIS BOOK FOR almost 30 years. After 15 years of teaching high school, I entered Duke Divinity School and eventually received my M. Div. and Ph.D. Throughout that educational process, I sought the answers to questions that troubled me about the relationship between the sacraments and my personal experience with Christ. I wrote many papers on the sacraments and then my doctoral dissertation (and first book) on baptism. Soon after, I was asked to serve on our denomination's Committee to Study Baptism. I wrote the final draft of that document, *By Water and the Spirit: Making Connections for Identity and Ministry*, and worked to get its understandings implemented. Then there was the Committee to Study Holy Communion. I was the primary writer of the document that was approved, *This Holy Mystery: A United Methodist Understanding of Holy Communion*. During the years of that process and since, I have been privileged to teach and preach about the sacraments many times in settings from seminary classes to pastors' school to Sunday school classes. I am pleased to be able to offer readers of this book the official teachings of The United Methodist Church and my own knowledge and experience of the sacraments.

It is my hope that this book will kindle renewed interest and appreciation of the sacraments as well as increased knowledge. Our lives in Christ are grounded in baptism and sustained by Eucharist. In baptism, God claims us for God's own and makes us members of Christ's body—the church. In baptism, God tells us who we are, for we are essentially nobody until we are in right relationship with God. In baptism, God gives us our life's ministry, for we are ignorant of our mission unless God shows us the meaning of life. In Holy Communion, God offers us grace ever new and more powerful. In Holy Communion, God gives us strength for our spiritual journey, for we cannot live as Christians in our own power. In Holy Communion, God makes us more holy, for we cannot become more like Christ through our efforts alone.

The chapters of this book are arranged in the hope of moving readers from understanding of what sacraments are to embodying and expressing sacramental grace in their lives. We are called to live baptism and Eucharist as well as receive them.

Chapter 1, "The Sacraments," explains the meaning of sacraments and why they are important to Christians. Here I state my conviction that recovery of our theological heritage is the key to spiritual revitalization in our time. Chapter 2, "Holy Baptism," deals with our lifelong process of salvation and the role of baptism in it. The United Methodist ritual for baptism is examined section by section. Chapter 3, "Questions About Baptism," deals with issues that, in my experience, almost always arise when a group of United Methodists talk about baptism.

Chapter 4, "Holy Communion," looks at the various meanings of the Lord's Supper and why it has not always been appreciated in Methodism, in spite of its great significance for our founder, John Wesley. The Eucharistic ritual is examined in an attempt to explain the meaning of its parts and how the service flows theologically. Chapter 5, "Questions About Holy Communion," is followed by another chapter based on my personal experiences of the questions that people have. It tries to answer some of these questions but concludes that some aspects must simply remain beyond our apprehension.

The book ends with Chapter 6, "Living as Baptized and Communing Christians." Here we consider the sacraments as instruments of God's radical equality and justice and how we are to live as sacramental people.

I want to thank the members of the committees to study baptism and Holy Communion for the opportunity to put their thoughts into words for the benefit of the church. I am also grateful for all of the people in my teaching sessions who have, in return, taught me. Above all, thanks to God whose love reaches us in sacrament.

—Gayle C. Felton

How to Use This Book

UNITED METHODISTS AND THE SACRAMENTS IS designed for use with any group of adults interested in learning more about how United Methodists understand and practice the sacraments of Holy Baptism and Holy Communion. This resource is ideal for use in new-member classes.

Each chapter includes reflection and discussion questions that will help the participants of a group identify and engage key questions and issues about baptism and Holy Communion. Such reflection can deepen faith and commitment to a Christian way of life. Each chapter also includes a simple leader guide that will help you lead your group. You will find suggestions for gathering supplies, setting up the space, hymns, and opening and closing prayers.

You can use this book in several different small-group formats. You may wish to use it in a small-group study that lasts six weeks. In this format, the group would read and discuss a chapter each session. You can also use the book in a study that has fewer sessions. For example, you could use Chapters 1 and 6 in the first session, Chapters 2 and 3 about baptism in the second session, and Chapters 4 and 5 about Holy Communion in the third session. Other combinations or arrangements of topics are also possible. Consider using the study book as a resource for a weekend retreat that includes meals, study, and worship experiences. How you read and discuss the chapters can be adapted to fit the needs of your local church.

The book can also be used for individual reading and reflection. Because it deals with United Methodist beliefs and practices related to the sacraments, it would be an ideal resource to place in a new-member packet.

We pray that UNITED METHODISTS AND THE SACRAMENTS will help all those who read and study it to experience transforming growth in faith and in living out the identity and mission of Christian life.

Chapter 1

The Sacraments

Here, O my Lord, I see thee face to face;
here would I touch and handle things
unseen;
here grasp with firmer hand eternal grace,
and all my weariness upon thee lean.[1]

W E HAVE SHOW-AND-TELL TOMORROW!" MANY
of us remember such words from our experience as children
or as parents. Can you recall how exciting it was to choose
an interesting object to take to school and then to be able to
tell classmates about it? Words alone would not have been
enough to communicate the unique importance of the
object. Simply holding it up for others to look at would have
been little fun. However, to show and tell, to demonstrate
and describe—that was wonderful! The sacraments of baptism and Holy Communion are God's show-and-tell.
Through them God offers us visible demonstration and
audible expression of God's love reaching out to us. There is
a country song that bemoans the plight of "looking for love
in all the wrong places." As Christians, we know where to
look for love; one of the right places is in the sacraments.

All of us search for something, or someone, that will give us a sense of meaning, an assurance of belonging, the certainty of acceptance. Many centuries ago, Saint Augustine addressed these needs by saying, "Thou hast made us for thyself and restless is our heart until it comes to rest in thee."[2] More recently, H. G. Wells spoke of a "God-shaped blank" in the innermost being of every person, an emptiness that God alone can fill.[3] I am convinced that a great deal of the dissatisfaction and turmoil that we experience and that we see in the lives of others is a result of the failure to allow that God-shaped space within to be filled by the one who created us and loves us unconditionally. The symptoms of pain and longing are everywhere: in broken relationships, in violence, in cheapened sex, in abuse of our bodies, in acquisition of possessions, in exploitation of the weak and rejection of the marginalized, in spiritual quests, and in emotional anguish. Some of this suffering is blatantly obvious; some of it is internally hidden.

All the substitutes with which we cram our lives as we seek meaning, belonging, and acceptance ultimately prove futile. The "God-shaped blank" remains. In *The Silver Chair*, one of the books in the series The Chronicles of Narnia, C. S. Lewis tells the story of a girl named Jill. Jill has been carried suddenly, by mysterious forces, into a strange land. She is frightened as she tries to get her bearings and decide what to do next. However, Jill's biggest problem, she soon realizes, is that she is desperately thirsty. Blessedly, she soon hears in the distance the enchanting sound of a running stream; and she runs toward it. As she emerges from the woods, Jill sees the glistening water just in front of her and starts to dash to it to quench her thirst. However, abruptly, Jill stops and freezes. Immediately in front of her, between her and the stream, lies an enormous golden lion. Jill is petrified. Readers of the Narnia Chronicles will recognize the lion as Aslan, the Christ-figure of the stories; but Jill sees only a dangerous beast. After a terrifying silence, the lion speaks to her.

" 'If you're thirsty, you may drink.' " And after no answer from Jill, " 'Are you not thirsty?' said the Lion.

'I'm dying of thirst,' said Jill.

'Then drink,' said the Lion. . . .

'Will you promise not to—do anything to me, if I do come?' said Jill.

'I make no promise,' said the Lion. . . .

'Do you eat girls?' she said.

'I have swallowed up girls and boys, women and men, kings and emperors, cities and realms,' said the Lion. . . .

'I daren't come and drink,' said Jill.

'Then you will die of thirst,' said the Lion.

'Oh dear!' said Jill, coming another step nearer. 'I suppose I must go and look for another stream then.'

'There is no other stream,' said the Lion."[4]

The lion's words are spoken to us. There is no other water to quench our thirsts, no other food to satisfy our hungers, except that grace that God offers through Jesus Christ. That is why the sacraments have relevance for us. They are channels through which the undeserved and unlimited love of God is made available to us.

What are some of the ways that people try to fill the "God-shaped blank" inside?

Sacrament—One of Those "Churchy" Words

Sacrament is not a word that we use much in our everyday speaking and writing. Even in the church, we are more likely to talk about baptism and the Lord's Supper than we are about sacraments. However, sacraments are so special that it is well worth our effort to grasp their meaning. Methodism's founder, John Wesley, following the teaching of the Anglican tradition, defined a *sacrament* as "an outward sign of inward grace, and a means whereby we receive the same."[5] So, first, a *sacrament* is something "outward"; it involves objects, actions, and people. It can be seen, felt, heard, and tasted. God has chosen things from the created world to use in sacraments. God uses these things—wheat, grapes, and water—as indicators of divine love; but this is just the beginning. When the Christian church uses these material things in special ways with special purposes, they become means by which we actually receive divine grace. This happens because God has chosen to act through them to channel God's active love to us. The water, wine or juice, and bread remain water, wine or juice, and bread; but they are consecrated or made holy by God's action through them.

Jesus Christ is an example of a sacrament. Jesus was a human being in and through whom God showed us the divine nature. The Christian church serves as a sacrament. It is made up of physical people and involves tangible things, and God works in and through it to fulfill God's purposes. What happens when the church celebrates a sacrament happens because of what God does. Something does happen, not because we "do it right" or can explain it but because these are ways in which God has decided to work.

This understanding of what a sacrament is and does is not something that John Wesley or we Methodists invented. Indeed, in general, this is the way sacraments are understood in most of the Christian bodies around the world, including Catholic, Orthodox, and Protestant. Sometimes, though, United Methodists get confused because of what they know about the practices and beliefs of some other Christian groups who place less emphasis on the sacraments. Perhaps the clearest example is Baptist churches. While they baptize and partake in the Lord's Supper, Baptists call these acts ordinances instead of sacraments. An *ordinance* is something that one performs in obedience to a command or a rule. Baptists baptize and commune because

Christ has commanded it. In ordinances, the emphasis is on what the individual or the community does; in sacraments, the emphasis is on what God does.[6]

How do you understand the word *sacrament?* How do you understand "an outward sign of inward grace"?

Neither Vending Machines nor Magic Wands

As we look more closely at the power and significance of the sacraments, it is important to note that they do not operate mechanically or magically. The church is not an arcade where a divine vending machine responds when we insert the correct coins or say the proper words with the proper actions. Our pastors are not robed magicians who can conjure up divine action by their incantations and gestures.

The Bible makes it clear that any movement of any kind that we can make toward God is only possible because God has already acted to make us able to do so. God always acts first; we can only respond. Our rituals for baptism and Holy Communion include, in the Prayer Over the Water and the Great Thanksgiving, summaries of the divine story of salvation or God's actions in history to make our salvation possible. Through the sacraments, God channels to each of us that same grace that has been at work in the past, is available today, and can be relied upon for tomorrow.

God's gifts to us, including the sacraments, are life-giving and life-changing. However, just like a gift to us from another person, divine gifts have to be accepted if they are to have meaning. If someone offers us a gift and we walk away refusing to accept it, the gift has no worth to us. Something valuable has been made available but has been refused. God deals with us in much the same way. We have been made creatures with free moral wills. We can make choices for or against good. We can accept or refuse what God offers us.

God works with human beings cooperatively, not forcibly. God offers and wants us to accept, but we must respond by willingly receiving. The grace made available to us in baptism and Holy Communion is a gift of God's outreaching love. It will not have automatic or magical results in our lives. We must first accept and utilize it.

How does the idea of sacraments as God's gifts speak to you? What other ways of thinking about sacraments occur to you?

Grace Is Grace Is Grace . . .

The word *grace* is used often in this book. The Methodist movement that issued in today's United Methodist Church is characterized by a central emphasis upon divine grace. The term is one we hear frequently in sermons, hymns, and prayers. What does it mean? Grace can be understood as God's free, undeserved favor toward us, in spite of our lack of merit. Grace is divine love working actively to appeal to us and to redeem us, even though we are unworthy. God's grace comes to us in many ways. The beauties of the natural world may reveal it. The love of family and friends shows its character. The lives of exemplary Christians model it. Sermons proclaim it. Grace is all around us if we are sensitive to its presence.

Grace is grace is grace; but in order to appreciate it better, we ought to explore the various ways that divine grace works in our lives through our salvation journey. It is essential to recognize that in Methodist theology, salvation is not an event; it is a process. Salvation is not a destination; it is a journey. All through our lives we travel on this spiritual journey—sometimes progressing but sometimes falling back. God's grace is always freely available to us, offering whatever we need at every point on the journey.

First, there is what Wesley called *prevenient grace.* This is the function of grace that "comes before." Prevenient grace restores our ability to make moral decisions; it enables us to be aware of God's calling us and to respond. Because of this work of grace, we are responsible (able to respond) and accountable for our choices.

Second, there is *justifying grace.* This work of grace forgives our sins and restores us to right relationship with God. Through justifying grace, we trust in Christ for salvation. Third, there is *sanctifying grace.* This work of grace is the work of regeneration through which we are spiritually born anew and launched on our journey of growth in holiness. Sanctifying grace empowers us to grow progressively into likeness to Christ. It is the process of turning more and more away from sin and becoming more consecrated, more holy, more the person whom God intends us to be. This perfecting grace ultimately transforms us so completely that we have no other motive in our lives except the love of God. Grace is grace is grace; but grace works in all of these ways, expressing itself differently as we find ourselves at different points in the process. God knows what work of grace we need even when we ourselves do not.

Methodism is a "means of grace" tradition. We acknowledge the presence of grace working in many ways; but we believe that there are certain means—channels, instruments—through which we can confidently anticipate receiving grace. It is somewhat like the wind: It blows wherever and whenever it wills; it touches people everywhere. Still, there are certain locations on the face of our planet where the winds can be confidently anticipated. These are the trade winds. We know where they are and from what direction they blow almost all the time. They can be relied upon. John Wesley taught that God's means of grace are like that. They can be relied upon. Wesley pointed out several of such means of grace: public worship, Bible reading and study, prayer, and fasting.[7] We have all probably experienced the reality of accessing grace through these practices.

Sacraments can be understood as especially powerful and dependable means of grace. They are never ways in which we attempt to earn salvation, for that is impossible. They are, instead, ways through which we are given what God wants us to have. Because God has chosen to so use them, baptism and Holy Communion convey God's transforming love to us most effectively. Because God has directed us to celebrate them, the sacraments can be trusted to fulfill the divine promise. There must never be a question of whether we *have to* practice baptism and Holy Communion. No, it is rather that we *get to* practice them. The sacraments are gifts from God. Why would we ever fail to celebrate them as fully and as often as we can?

What means of grace have been most helpful to you in your life of faith? How do you understand the difference between "have to practice" and "get to practice" when it comes to the sacraments?

How Many Sacraments?

We are aware that Roman Catholic and Eastern Orthodox churches have seven sign-acts that they practice as sacraments: Holy Baptism, Confirmation/Chrismation; Mass/Eucharist; Penance/Reconciliation; Marriage; Ordination; and Healing/Last Rites.[8] The Protestant reformers who led the breakaway from Roman Catholicism in the 16th century reduced this number to two. In general, they believed that a sacrament is a sign-act that had been instituted by Christ during his earthly life and to which a divine promise is connected. New Testament texts can be cited as validation. For example, in Mark 16:16, the risen Christ says to his disciples, "The one who believes and is baptized will be saved" Similarly, in

Matthew 28:18-20, Jesus says, "Go therefore and make disciples of all nations, baptizing them in the name of the Father and of the Son and of the Holy Spirit.... And remember, I am with you always, to the end of the age."

For Holy Communion, a validating text is Matthew 26:26-29: "While they were eating, Jesus took a loaf of bread, and after blessing it he broke it, gave it to the disciples, and said, 'Take eat; this is my body.' Then he took a cup, and after giving thanks he gave it to them, saying, 'Drink from it, all of you; for this is my blood of the covenant, which is poured out for many for the forgiveness of sins. I tell you, I will never again drink of this fruit of the vine until that day when I drink it new with you in my Father's kingdom.'" Almost all Protestant churches continue to recognize only baptism and Holy Communion as sacraments, arguing that these two alone have the authority of "dominical (by the Lord) institution."

Our recognition of only two ritual actions as sacraments does not mean that United Methodists deny the importance of other services that mark the need for and the reception of divine grace at various points in our lives. Indeed, there is growing emphasis on the celebration of additional rituals. In *The United Methodist Hymnal*, there is a significant service for "Congregational Reaffirmation of Baptism," which will be discussed more in a later chapter. Further evidence can be seen in *The United Methodist Book of Worship*, which features a variety of services for life occasions. Examples are A Celebration of New Beginnings in Faith and An Order for Commitment to Christian Service in the Occasional Services section. Part VIII of the *Book of Worship* is composed of Healing Services and Prayers appropriate for healing in general and for times of individual and family crisis.

Baptism is a sacrament that initiates us into the church, the body of Christ. Holy Communion is a sacrament that sustains and nurtures us in our journey of faith. Other rituals deepen our commitment, strengthen our faith, and allow us to consecrate our lives to God. Confirmation is the occasion on which a person who was baptized as an infant professes his or her own faith by taking the vows before the congregation. Through this profession of faith, the baptized member becomes a professing member of the church. (Persons who are baptized as adults profess their faith through taking the vows on the same occasion as their baptism and become baptized and professing members.) Confession of sin and reconciliation are offered at the beginning of services of the Lord's Supper but are also needed throughout life as we fail to be faithful to our side of the baptismal covenant.

While we do not consider marriage to be a sacrament, certainly it celebrates a commitment that requires God's grace and can be a source of that grace. The ordination of deacons and elders as clergy is an occasion on which we emphasize the workings of the gracious Holy Spirit. For lay people, an equivalent would be their consecration to whatever work of service God has called them. The importance of healing amid the brokenness of our lives has already been mentioned. Some people advocate for the practice of footwashing, particularly since Jesus said to the disciples, "You ought also to wash one another's feet" (John 13:14b).

At the end of life, rituals with the dying and at burials or interments offer divine grace for thanksgiving and comfort. None of the rituals that mark these life occasions are considered to be sacraments in the full meaning of that term: words, elements, and actions used as vehicles of divine grace to fulfill Christ's commands and claim God's promises. They are better thought of as "sacramental"—additional means of grace available through all of life.

What services or rituals in addition to the sacraments of baptism and Holy Communion have been meaningful to you or occasions when you have experienced God's grace?

Revival Through Recovery

In United Methodism's current hymnal, the services of baptism and Holy Communion appear at the front of the book. This is a change in their traditional position in Methodist hymnals, a change made by the General Conference, our denomination's highest authority. It is not an editorial decision; it is a theological statement. It indicates the recovery in our church of the centrality of the sacraments in Christian history and in the Methodist heritage.

The Church of England (Anglican) is the direct parent of the Methodist movement and the denominations that have developed from it. This means that United Methodism's closest relative in the family tree of churches is the Episcopal Church. This formal worship, sacramental tradition was brought together by John Wesley with an evangelical and revivalistic passion. Methodism is a blend or balance of these two emphases; neither alone is authentic.

During its history in America, Methodism has not always been able to sustain this balance between the two parts of our heritage. Especially during the evangelistic enthusiasm of the 19th century, the sacraments were sometimes devalued although never abandoned. By the early 20th century, Methodism was moving away from the evangelical aspect of its heritage as stress upon conversion diminished. Having then neglected the sacramental and evangelical aspects of its tradition, Methodism struggled for a sense of identity and mission. I am convinced that a significant cause of our current problems and decline in membership is because we no longer know who we are and what mission we have been called to.

By the mid-20th century, our appreciation of the sacraments had shriveled to the point of distortion. Infant baptism was considered to be a service in which parents dedicated themselves to appropriate nurture and education of the child. Adult baptism was viewed as a service of joining the church. Holy Communion was practiced as a solemn memorial of the death of Christ.

By the 1960's, church records showed evidence of concern over this loss of sacramental appreciation and the beginning of attempts to recover. The services of the Baptismal Covenant and of Word and Table in our current hymnal are the result of the effort to guide the church toward reclaiming its sacramental roots. The same General Conference that approved our hymnal in 1988 directed the creation of a committee to study baptism and to present a document to the church. *By Water and the Spirit: A United Methodist Understanding of Baptism* was approved by General Conference in 1996 as the church's official interpretive and teaching document on this sacrament.[9] The 2004 General Conference approved another document, the product of a similar committee's work, *This Holy Mystery: A United Methodist Understanding of Holy Communion*.[10] We now have, for the first time in our history, comprehensive officially approved statements of how United Methodism understands and practices the sacraments. Ongoing study of these documents, of which this book is a part, will enable us to recapture the significance of this vital aspect of our heritage.[11]

This revitalization of our sacramental tradition does not mean that we should or will diminish our evangelical emphasis. Indeed, I believe that it will enable us to rekindle that part of our heritage as well. The sacraments offer us divine grace, but this gift of grace must be accepted by persons whose hearts and wills are being opened to transformation by Christ through the Holy Spirit. Personal relationship with the Christ who is saving us is empowered through the grace we receive in the sacraments.

What indications do you see in your church that the significance of the sacraments is being recovered?

SUGGESTIONS FOR THE GROUP SESSION

Gather Supplies

Several copies of *The United Methodist Hymnal* and *The Faith We Sing*; Bibles; large sheets of paper or poster paper and pens; other research resources such as *Word and Table*; *By Water and the Spirit: A United Methodist Understanding of Baptism*; *This Holy Mystery: A United Methodist Understanding of Holy Communion*; *The Interpreter's Dictionary of the Bible*; *The United Methodist Book of Worship*; *The Book of Discipline of The United Methodist Church, 2004*; *The Book of Resolutions of The United Methodist Church, 2004*; and *The Oxford Dictionary of the Christian Church*.

Arrange the Learning Area

Ahead of time write each of the following words on a sheet of newsprint—one to a sheet—and post them on a wall or other easily visible location.

"Sacraments"
"Grace"
"Means of Grace"

Lead the Session

- Open the session with a prayer for God's guidance as the group explores the meaning of the sacraments.
- Invite participants to write on the sheets of newsprint any questions they have about the words written there.
- Read the sections in the chapter using the questions at the end to stimulate discussion. Use the newsprint lists to stimulate further discussion for each of the sections.

- Sing or read the first stanza of "Here, O My Lord, I See Thee" (*The United Methodist Hymnal*, 623).
- Close the session with a prayer offering thanks to God for the gift of grace and presence through the sacraments.

Chapter 2

Baptism: Identity and Mission

We your people stand before you,
water-washed and Spirit-born.
By your grace, our lives we offer.
Recreate us; God transform![1]

God Claims Us

WHO ARE WE? WHAT ARE WE SUPPOSED TO BE doing? These questions could be worded much more eloquently; but regardless of how expressed, they probe at the heart of human experience. We all want confidence about who we are—within ourselves, in relation to others, and in relation to the power that is the foundation of the universe. We seek these things through other people, through work, through religion, through psychotherapy, to name a few. There seems to be a universal need to find out what we should be doing. We ask young children, "What do you want to do when you grow up?" In school and at home we urge them to consider their vocational choices. Many of us change jobs frequently during our working years, perhaps pushed by a nagging sense that we are not doing the right thing. We also wonder how we are to spend our retired years.

The Christian faith offers us answers, not necessarily in detailed precision but certainly in self-knowledge and direction sufficient to be the foundation of our lives. Baptism provides us with an identity and our mission. When God claims us in baptism, God tells us who we are. We are precious creations of God, valued beyond our comprehension, and loved throughout all circumstances and events. We belong to God; that is who we are. In his book on baptism, *Remember Who You Are: Baptism, a Model for Christian Life*, Will Willimon emphasizes that our baptismal identity is so real that it has the power to determine the remainder of our lives.[2]

When God claims us in baptism, God tells us what we are to do. To be baptized is to be sent on a mission, to be assigned a ministry or service. Baptism can be thought of as ordination to ministry. We are set apart for the work of Christ's church, the continuation of the effort to redeem the world. Of course, this does not mean that all of us are to be clergy. The point is rather that all ministry has its roots in baptism and that every life work for a Christian is to be one to which we have been commissioned by God. We are whom God tells us we are, and we are to be doing what God tells us to do. It is that simple and that profound.

How do you respond to the questions about identity and mission? Who are you? What is your mission?

Is Baptism Really That Important?

When I was working on my dissertation on the practice and theology of baptism in American Methodism, the research and writing went on and on. The resources to be consulted were voluminous, many of them fragile and yellowed by age. My research took so long that at one point my supportive mother looked at me and asked, "Gayle, what can you possibly be doing this long? Is baptism really that important?" Probably many people in the church wonder the same thing. Let me try to explain why I believe baptism is so important.

Baptism connects to every other aspect of the Christian faith and offers insight into all theology. The sacrament reveals to us the nature and purpose of God who seeks us out and claims us for God's own. Baptism makes clear our nature as human beings who are in need of divine grace. Baptism is part of the process of salvation through which our right relationship is restored and through which we become the people God intends. Baptism initiates us into the church, which serves as Christ's body in God's ongoing work. Baptism enables us to face our own deaths with assurance and to anticipate the final end of the age in the certainty of divine victory. In baptism, the gospel is heard, seen, and felt.

How does baptism connect to your life and faith? How does it speak to you about the gospel of God's saving love in Jesus Christ?

Is Baptism Essential? Is it Sufficient?

John Wesley emphasized the importance of baptism: "In the ordinary way, there is no other means of entering into the Church or into heaven."[3] This statement makes apparent the immense significance of the sacrament as the way that God has chosen to initiate persons into God's realm. It demands that we take baptism with utmost seriousness, recognizing that it is not a human invention but a gift of God. Yet at the same time, Wesley's description of baptism as "the ordinary channel" indicates that there are other less ordinary means through which God works. God is always radically free and operates however and wherever God chooses. God is the giver of the sacraments and intends that we use them but is not limited to working through them. This is why baptism in not absolutely essential to salvation. If we do not accept and use the divine gift as it is intended, God finds other ways to communicate grace. God cannot be limited by our failures. This does not excuse our negligence or disobedience. It simply means that God can and does work in spite of them.

Neither is baptism sufficient for salvation. The sacrament is only a part—although an important part—of the process of salvation that goes on throughout the lives of Christian people. Remember there is nothing either mechanical or magical about the sacraments. There is no "dipped and done" or "sprinkled and succeeded" aspect to baptism, no ticket to heaven issued, no guarantee of goodness. When *By Water and the Spirit: A United Methodist Understanding of Baptism* was being discussed before and at General Conference, there were those who opposed it because they believed that it placed too much stress on the spiritual benefits of baptism. They feared that if baptism were restored to its previously prominent place in Methodist theology and practice, the significance of personal commitment to Christ might be devalued. They viewed the relationship between the two aspects of authentic Methodism—the sacramental and the evangelical—as existing on a seesaw, so that if one side went up, then the other necessarily went down. This is simply not the case. No matter the importance of baptism, it is not the end of the salvation story. The grace that God bestows in the sacrament must be received and responded to by the baptized person. Baptism is profoundly evangelical because it portrays the outreaching love of God being offered and the human response of faith and commitment.

What is your view of the connection between salvation and baptism?

The Journey

The Christian life is often described as a journey. Perhaps *The Pilgrim's Progress* is the best-known example. This understanding is foundational to the thought of John Wesley and to the theology of United Methodism. Unlike some Christians, then and now, Wesley never believed that humanity was divided into the saved and unsaved. Instead, he taught that all of us are at some point in the ongoing process of salvation. Our place in the journey changes: Sometimes we are moving forward, sometimes sliding back. Because we have freedom to make moral decisions and respond positively or negatively to divine grace, we determine our progress on the journey.

The grace of baptism is not an end in itself; it is rather a crucial means of further spiritual growth. Baptism makes a person a member of the church. The church functions as a school of faith. Within that community, we learn what it means to be Christian and how to shape our lives on the model of Christ's life. For an infant or a young child, the sacrament begins a process of nurture and formation with the goal of enabling the child to make his or her own commitment to Christ. This commitment is made before the congregation when the baptized person, having reached an age of moral accountability, professes her or his faith by answering the vows in the service of confirmation. Adults are baptized and confirmed on the same occasion. However, like children, their baptism should follow and be followed by ongoing nurture in the beliefs and practices of Christianity and shaping in holiness of life.

How do you respond to the image of journey as a way of talking about Christian life and faith? How do you see the connection between baptism and the Christian journey?

Our Baptismal Liturgy

If we listen carefully to the words used in our baptismal services and observe closely the actions, all of the above points about the meaning of the sacrament are expressed. Perhaps if we examine the service here in more detail, it will deepen our appreciation when we participate in the future.

Service I of The Services of the Baptismal Covenant includes all five aspects of the ritual: Holy Baptism, Confirmation, Reaffirmation, Reception Into The United Methodist Church, and Reception Into the Congregation.[4] It will be fruitful to use the study edition of *By Water and the Spirit* along with the material here, so the appropriate pages of that document will be noted at the end of the session. The study edition also contains a copy of the service through which you can follow the sections being discussed.[5]

Note first the title of the ritual: Services of the Baptismal *Covenant*. This is an important term for our understanding of the sacrament. It establishes a covenant between God and us. A covenant is a two-sided agreement involving promises and responsibilities on the part of both parties. The idea of covenant is important in the Bible. The Old Testament is the story of God's covenant with the Hebrew people. God promised to be their God and to make them God's people. The Hebrews (Israelites) promised to obey God's commands and allow God to work through their history. The sign of that covenant was and is circumcision. The New Testament is the story of Jesus Christ and the covenant that his life, death, and resurrection make possible between God and the Christian church. God promises restored relationship, new life, and ultimately the transformation of the created world. Christians accept divine grace and pledge to become co-workers with God in this work of redemption. The sign of this covenant is baptism.[6]

Section 1 is the introduction to the service and should always be used to open the ritual. It indicates immediately that baptism is not a private or an individualistic service. Note that the pronouns in this section are plural: "Through the Sacrament of Baptism *we* are initiated into Christ's holy church. / *We* are incorporated into God's mighty acts of salvation and given new birth through water and the Spirit. / All this is God's gift, offered to *us* without price."[7] Initiation is into the church and into the divine work for human salvation. For this reason, baptism should always be administered within a congregational worship service, unless unusual circumstances make it impossible. It is an act of God through the gathered community of faith functioning as the body of Christ.[8]

If confirmation or reaffirmation is to be part of the service, Section 2 follows. This section would not be included if only infants and young children are being baptized because they are not confirmed until later in life. It is important if adults are being baptized, professing their faith, or transferring into the congregation. Emphasis here is on the human response of faith and the need for us to renew and rededicate ourselves: "We renew the covenant declared at our baptism, / acknowledge what God is doing for us, / and affirm our commitment to Christ's holy church."[9]

Section 3 is the point at which individuals are called by name and presented to the congregation of which they are (if already baptized) or are becoming a member. It is an informal time when the lay leader or sponsors can make brief remarks to help the congregation get to know the individuals. Leadership by laypersons here emphasizes the congregation, not just clergy who are heard and seen most.

One of the most significant parts of the service is Section 4, which is called Renunciation of Sin and Profession of Faith.[10] It should be used in every service of the baptismal covenant whether baptism, confirmation, reaffirmation, or reception.

The questions are answered by persons able to speak for themselves and by the parents or guardians and sponsors of infants being baptized. (Note that parents, guardians, or sponsors are not speaking for the child; they are professing their own faith.) The first question is a negative one asking for a change of loyalty: "On behalf of the whole church, I ask you: / Do you renounce the spiritual forces of wickedness, / reject the evil powers of this world, / and repent of your sin?"[11] It recognizes the reality of evil at the cosmic, systemic, and personal levels. In some of the baptismal services of the early Christian church, persons literally turned around and faced an opposite direction to express their attitude toward evil.

The second question implies that God has conquered wickedness and asks us to accept the ability to oppose it also: "Do you accept the freedom and power God gives you / to resist evil, injustice, and oppression / in whatever forms they present themselves?"[12] The power of wickedness is not vague or abstract. It is manifested in our daily experiences and interactions. It must be watched for and actively opposed when it is found. To commit ourselves to do that is to promise to stand against those persons and things that are wrong and make intentional efforts to improve the lives of all people.

The third profession asks us to declare trust or faith in Christ. This is not simply a statement of belief. It is a pledge to devote our lives to service as part of the church: "Do you confess Jesus Christ as your Savior, / put your whole trust in his grace, / and promise to serve him as your Lord, / in union with the church which Christ has opened / to people of all ages, nations, and races?"[13] The last words indicate the inclusiveness of the authentic church of Christ. It welcomes all persons who profess Christian faith. It imposes no barriers against any who wish to join; its welcome is as wide as is the love of its Lord.

In what ways can the vows in Section 4, Renunciation of Sin and Profession of Faith, be lived out in daily life?

Section 5 is used if the service involves infants or young children or in cases in which persons of any age are unable to answer for themselves due to physical or mental limitations. The question is addressed to the parents, guardians, or sponsors who have professed their faith by making the previous vows: "Will you nurture *these children* (*persons*) / in Christ's holy church, / that by your teaching and example they may be guided / to accept God's grace for themselves, / to profess their faith openly, / and to lead a Christian life?"[14] At least one parent or guardian should be a member of a Christian church. Otherwise, how could they honestly take the vows? Sponsors may or may not be called godparents. They are mature Christians who pledge to help raise the child in the faith. All of these responsible adults promise to teach and live Christianity for these children. The goal of this nurture is to prepare baptized children, once they have reached an appropriate age, to be ready to profess their personal faith by taking the vows in the service we call confirmation.

A two-fold pledge is made in Section 6: "According to the grace given you, / will you remain *faithful members* of Christ's holy church / and serve as Christ's *representatives* in the world?"[15] Candidates for baptism, confirmation, or reaffirmation promise faithfulness to the church. Some particular ways of doing this have already been voiced in the earlier vows, and others will be specified later. Persons also take on the awesome responsibility of being representatives of Christ in the world, living advertisements for Christianity, doing what Christ would have done.

Section 7 recognizes the value of having sponsors for persons who can answer for themselves, as well as for those who cannot. Adults who are coming into the church today often were not raised in the Christian faith and have little background in the church. The commitment of these people to Christ may be strong, but they can greatly benefit from the guidance and example of more mature Christians. Even those who have grown up in the church need Christian companions and mentors as they seek to live out their faith. In the pledge in Section 7, those chosen as sponsors take on that responsibility.

What are the benefits to baptized persons of having godparents or sponsors?

Every service of the baptismal covenant is an opportunity for the whole congregation to reassert its own Christian commitment: "Do you, as Christ's body, the church, / reaffirm both your rejection of sin / and your commitment to Christ?"[16] The congregational response in Section 8 is a promise to the church and to the persons being baptized, confirmed, and reaffirmed. This response emphasizes that the faith is not normally lived out in isolation but in community with other Christians: "Will you nurture one another in the Christian faith and life and include *these persons* now before you in your care?"[17] It is in a community of love and forgiveness that Christians are best enabled to grow in faith, service, and discipleship: "With God's help we will proclaim the good news / and live according to the example of Christ. / We will surround *these persons* / with a community of love and forgiveness / and *they* may grow in *their* trust of God, / and be found faithful in *their* service to others. / We will pray for *them*, / that *they* may be true disciples who walk in the way that leads to life."[18]

The use of the Apostles' Creed in services of baptism, Section 9, is an ancient practice going back to the early centuries of the church. While it had not been used in this way in Methodist services since the 1930s, its restoration is important. Use of the creed places the faith proclamation of individuals and congregations today within the universal Christian church through time. The question and answer arrangement is traditional. The portions enclosed in brackets are not required in order to meet membership requirements but should be used unless there are unusual circumstances. The version of the creed here is slightly different from that most familiar to United Methodists. It is a modern translation used by Protestant denominations and Roman Catholics.

When baptisms or reaffirmations are being celebrated, water is poured into the font. Fonts differ in size and location, but arrangement should allow for the water to be seen and heard. The beautiful prayer of Thanksgiving Over the Water in Section 10 is comparable to the Great Thanksgiving in the service of Holy Communion. Its theme is the role of water in God's mighty acts of salvation in the past: "Eternal Father: / when nothing existed but chaos, / you swept across the dark waters / and brought forth light. / In the days of Noah / you saved those on the ark through water. / After the flood you set in the clouds a rainbow. / When you saw your people as slaves in Egypt, / you led them to freedom through the sea. / Their children you brought through the Jordan / to the land which you promised."[19] Clearly the greatest of God's works: "In the fullness of time you sent Jesus, / nurtured in the water of a womb. / He was baptized by John and anointed by your Spirit. / He called his disciples / to share in the baptism of his death and resurrection / and to make disciples of all nations."[20] At the conclusion of the prayer, the Holy Spirit is called: "Pour out your Holy Spirit, / to bless this gift of water and *those* who *receive* it, / to wash away *their* sin / and clothe *them* in righteousness / throughout *their* lives, / that, dying and being raised with Christ, / *they* may share in his final victory"[21] At four points in the prayer, the whole worshiping community praises God in joyous congregational responses spoken or sung.

What are some of our associations with water that might help us appreciate its meaning in baptism?

In Section 11, each candidate is baptized individually in the name of the Father, Son, and Holy Spirit, in accord with Matthew 28:19. (Other terms for the Trinity that would not speak of God as male have been suggested, but none has yet become widely accepted. This continues to be a challenge for the church as we seek to express the full nature of God and the equal likeness of both genders to God.) Water is used for sprinkling, pouring, or immersion. Often water is applied three times to symbolize the triune nature of God. Only the given names, not surnames, of persons are spoken, since they are being initiated into the family of the church rather than a human family. The laying on of hands, on a person's head or shoulders, is an ancient practice of the church that indicates the receiving of the Holy Spirit. Family members, including baptized children, and sponsors are invited to participate as the pastor says, "The Holy Spirit work within you, / that being born through water and the Spirit, / you may be a faithful disciple of Jesus Christ."[22] The response of "Amen" here and elsewhere in the ritual is affirmation by the congregation of what has been done and said. *The United Methodist Book of Worship* suggests several other actions that can be meaningful at this point in the service. The sign of the cross may be traced on the forehead as an indication of God's seal placed upon us in baptism. Using oil to make this cross emphasizes the identity of Christians as a royal priesthood, as in 1 Peter 2:9. New clothing, as a symbol of putting on Christ for new life, may be presented. A baptismal candle may be given as a reminder that Christians are to let our light be seen by the world. This candle can be used in the home as a part of the celebration of anniversaries of the baptism. Pastors should prepare a certificate of baptism and present it at this point or after the service. In the words of welcome closing this section, the congregation expresses its joy and unity with the new members of the community of faith: "Through baptism / you are incorporated by the Holy Spirit / into God's new creation / and made to share in Christ's royal priesthood. / We are all one in Christ Jesus. / With joy and thanksgiving we welcome you / as *members* of the family of Christ."[23]

Sections 12 and 13, Confirmation or Reaffirmation of Faith,[24] are part of the baptisms of persons able to answer for themselves, for they need no separate service of confirmation. They are also for persons who were baptized as infants and are now ready to profess their faith and in reaffirmations. Water is used here in order to stress the connections to baptism, but care must be taken not to appear to be repeating the sacrament. Water is a symbol reminding us of our baptism. It can be simply seen and heard, touched, used to make the sign of the cross, or sprinkled toward the congregation. To "remember your baptism and be thankful"[25] is not to recall the event itself. It is to reclaim the meaning of baptism and the divine grace that continues to work in our lives.

Confirmation is best understood as a person's first reaffirmation of baptismal vows. There are at least three meanings of the service. First, God confirms the divine promise to those who were too young to grasp what God was doing in their baptism. Second, the persons publicly profess their own faith in Christ and confirm their acceptance of the grace that they have received. In a sense, they are confirming the faith of their parents, saying, "Yes, this is who I want to be, who I was made in baptism." Finally, the church as represented by this congregation confirms the commitments the persons are making and its own support. Confirmation includes the laying on of hands that, unlike baptism, is an action that is properly repeated. The words said by the pastor are the same as those following baptism, except for a change in the tense of the verb. "That having been born through water and the Spirit"[26] indicates that spiritual rebirth has already taken place.

Why is profession of faith or confirmation so important in a person's spiritual development?

Confirmation is not the last occasion for reaffirming our faith. Indeed, it is simply the first. Recognizing this frees us from so much concern about the proper age for confirmation. Throughout our lives, we need to renew our trust in Christ and recommit ourselves to be faithful to the church's mission. We need intentional opportunities to participate in individual and communal services of reaffirmation. Baptismal Covenant IV[27] is a powerful new service of reaffirmation that congregations are finding to be deeply meaningful.

What value do you see in regular services of reaffirmation of baptismal vows?

Reception into The United Methodist Church, Section 14,[28] follows confirmations and baptisms of persons able to answer for themselves. It is also for receiving as United Methodists persons who are baptized members of other Christian denominations. The question is, "As members of Christ's universal church, will you be loyal to The United Methodist Church, and do all in your power to strengthen its ministries?"[29]

Professing members—those who have been baptized and confirmed—along with those transferring from other local United Methodist congregations are received into this congregation in Section 15. All baptized and confirmed United Methodists are professing members of the denomination and of a particular local congregation.

In Section 16, the pastor approvingly presents to the congregation all persons who have taken any of the steps described in the previous ritual. The pastor reminds the congregation of their duties to "do all in your power to increase *their* faith, / confirm *their* hope, and perfect *them* in love."[30] The congregation responds with thanks, welcome, and reaffirmation: "As members together with you / in the body of Christ / and in this congregation / of The United Methodist Church, / we renew our covenant / faithfully to participate in the ministries of the church by our prayer, our presence, our gifts, and our service, that in everything God may be glorified through Jesus Christ."[31] Church membership is not something we experience alone; it places us in a family of faith where together we grow in holiness, worship God, and serve others.

SUGGESTIONS FOR THE GROUP SESSION

Gather Supplies

Several copies of *The United Methodist Hymnal* and *The Faith We Sing*; Bibles; large sheets of paper or poster paper and pens; *By Water and the Spirit: A United Methodist Understanding of Baptism*; *This Holy Mystery: A United Methodist Understanding of Holy Communion*; *The Interpreter's Dictionary of the Bible*; *The United Methodist Book of Worship*; *The Book of Discipline of The United Methodist Church, 2004*; *The Book of Resolutions of The United Methodist Church, 2004*; and *The Oxford Dictionary of the Christian Church.*

Arrange the Learning Area

• Write the question "Who are we?" on a large sheet of paper. Write the question "What are we supposed to be doing?" on a second large sheet of paper. Post these on a wall or other easily visible location.

• Make sure everyone has a place to sit. Arrange the room to make discussion easier.

Lead the Session

• Pour the water in the pitcher into the bowl. Invite participants to listen to the water. After a moment of silence, pray together for any needs in the group and for God's guidance as you explore baptism and our identity and mission as members of God's beloved family.

• Invite participants to write responses to the questions "Who are we?" and "What are we supposed to be doing?" on the large pieces of paper you have posted.

• Read or summarize in your own words each of the following sections: "God Claims Us," "Is Baptism Really That Important?" "Is Baptism Essential? Is it Sufficient?" and "The Journey." Ask the questions at the end of these sections to stimulate discussion.

• Give group members a copy of *The United Methodist Hymnal*, and ask them turn to 32. Invite them to look at each section of The Baptismal Covenant I as you review "Our Baptismal Liturgy." Ask the questions throughout this section to stimulate discussion. Invite any other questions that group members may have about the liturgy.

• Read or sing stanzas 1 and 3 of "Wash, O God, Our Sons and Daughters" (*Hymnal*, 605).

• Close the session by offering a prayer of thanksgiving that through baptism God claims us and calls us to mission.

Chapter 3

Questions About Baptism

Baptized in water, sealed by the Spirit,
cleansed by the blood of Christ, our King;
heirs of salvation, trusting his promise,
faithfully now God's praises we sing.[1]

IF MY EXPERIENCES OF DISCUSSING BAPTISM WITH many different groups are an indication, there are, indeed, people who have questions about baptism. They also have criticisms, complaints, confusion, and disagreements. The subject is one that arouses many memories and opinions. Not surprisingly, Methodists have had debates about baptismal issues throughout our history. Some have been disputes with other denominational groups whose theology and practices differed from ours. Others have been within the Methodist family as diverse understandings and actions emerged.

What About Believer's Baptism?

In the 19th century, the sharpest competitors with Methodism on the ever-moving western frontier were the

Baptists and the Campbellites (who developed into the Disciples of Christ). The degree of antagonism that existed may be unexpected to us, but it is fair to say that the propaganda was similar to that of political campaigns. Both groups practiced only believer's baptism and were often harshly critical of what they termed "baby-sprinkling." Baptists and Campbellites understood baptism to be the public profession of faith made by a person who had decided to commit his or her life to Christ. As such, baptism could only be received by adults—those who had attained an age of moral accountability. In such a view, the baptism of infants and young children was meaningless and could not be considered baptism at all. Persons who had been baptized as infants in traditions such as Methodism were required to be baptized as adults if they wished to join a Baptist or a Campbellite church. This was necessary not because such persons needed to be "re-baptized" but because they had never been truly baptized at all.

In believer's baptism traditions, baptism is viewed as an ordinance, not a sacrament. It is something that is done to fulfill a command to Christ. It is primarily an action of the individual Christian who is professing faith before the gathered community of the congregation. The church is understood as being made up of committed believers who have so declared themselves by receiving baptism. This view of baptism is significantly different from the United Methodist understanding described in Chapters 1 and 2. In our sacramental theology, the chief actor in baptism is not a person; it is God. God acts regardless of the age of the person receiving the sacrament. It sometimes seems to me that these two understandings of what both call baptism are so different that it might be helpful if we had different names for them. Because we do not, the difference causes considerable confusion. Many United Methodists are influenced by the positions and practices of their believer's-baptism neighbors and, therefore, find it hard to understand fully and appreciate those of their own church.

How do you understand the difference between infant and believer's baptism?

What About Infant Baptism?

When I was growing up in a small town in eastern North Carolina, I was puzzled and a little embarrassed about the baptism of infants in my Methodist congregation. The practice seemed odd; it was only performed by a few Methodists and Presbyterians in the community. The majority of Baptists—virtually the whole world, it seemed to me—rejected it and baptized only adult believers. It was well into my adult life when broadening educational opportunities enabled me to learn that infant baptism has been the almost universal practice of the church of Jesus Christ for 2,000 years.

We know that early Christian baptisms in the New Testament period often included whole families (Acts 2:38-41; 16:15, 33.) While it is never stated explicitly, some of them almost surely contained infants and young children. There is no New Testament mention of an age requirement for baptism nor is there an account of a person who grew up in a Christian home being baptized as an adult. In the Jewish community where Christianity had its birth, infants (males) were received into the covenant community through circumcision when they were eight days old. It is logical to believe that Jewish Christians administered baptism, the sign of the new covenant, to their babies to initiate them into the community of faith. Certainly there is historical evidence of infant baptism as far back as the early Christian centuries.[2]

Far more important are the theological ideas supporting the baptism of infants. All of us, of any age, depend on the loving acceptance of God for our salvation. None are wise enough or can work hard enough to earn right relationship with God. Indeed, we all come before God as helpless sinners in need of God's grace. We are loved and accepted by God when we can do nothing to save ourselves. When the person being baptized is an infant, this truth is made undeniably clear. God claims babies from the beginning of their lives. They are brought into the church, the community of faith, by baptism. In the church, they learn how to be Christians as they are shaped by teaching and example.

Baptism is a part of this process of growing and learning in commitment to Christ and to the church. Therefore, it may not be appropriate for all babies. Our ritual says that at least one parent, guardian, or sponsor should be "a member of Christ's holy church." Also parents should bring their children for baptism for the right reasons. People who seek the sacrament for their children because it is "the thing to do," to satisfy the wishes of grandparents or other relatives, or for other trivial reasons may not be able to take the vows in honesty. Most likely, they will not be able to nurture the child in the faith at home and in church. In such situations, baptism may need to be postponed.

Some people think of christening as a separate or different service than baptism, but it is the same thing. The use of the word *christening* for the sacrament probably comes from two sources. First, *chrism* is the name of the anointing oil traditionally used in baptism as a sign of the Holy Spirit. Second, in the past children were sometimes actually given their (Christian) names in baptism. In our present ritual, parents are not asked for the name of the child; but the pastor does baptize with that name without using the family or surname. This meaning of christening is expressed, for example, in a ceremony for the naming of a ship. Unfortunately, the term has sometimes been used as a way of diminishing the significance of infant baptism or of indicating that it is something different from and less than the baptism of an adult. Such a view is inconsistent with United Methodist understanding of baptism.

Is dedication an option? No, United Methodist parents do not have a choice between baptism and dedication for their infants because the theological understanding of the two services is different. Dedication is a human act, something we pledge or give to God. Baptism is a divine act, something God promises and gives to us. The baptism of an infant includes the dedication of the child and of the parents, the recognition that the child belongs to God and the promise to nurture and form the child in the Christian faith. (See especially Section 5 of the ritual.) However, baptism chiefly celebrates what God is doing and what God will do. United Methodists practice infant baptism because of the way that we understand God's grace to work. Pastors are directed in the *Book of Discipline* to "earnestly exhort" parents to have their infants baptized. Pastors and congregations should provide appropriate teaching to enable parents to understand the significance of the sacrament and seek it for their children.

How do you understand infant baptism? What are some ways that family members and the church community can nurture a child's faith?

What About Emergency Baptism?

For centuries, the Roman Catholic Church taught that babies who died without having received baptism could not enter into heaven and be with God. This harsh belief was based on the understanding that all persons are born into the world carrying a burden of original sin and guilt that separates them from God. This sin and guilt is removed by baptism; but if baptism is not received and the child dies, right relationship to God cannot be restored. Somehow, this ancient Roman Catholic doctrine (which the Catholic

Church no longer teaches) has crept into the thought of many Protestant people, including United Methodists.

Indeed, it has become a widespread folk belief that baptism is necessary to ensure a dying child's eternal destiny. Truly it is more a superstition than a doctrine. It is what drives parents of a seriously ill newborn to call for a pastor to come to baptize the child immediately. Worse, it is what motivates hospital personnel to administer the sacrament themselves if a clergy person is not available. In Roman Catholicism, this is called "emergency baptism." In United Methodism, there is no such thing as emergency baptism because there is no emergency. We believe that God's loving care surrounds and accepts all dying children. Receiving the sacrament does not change the eternal destiny of the child.

This is not to say that there are not circumstances in which a terminally ill infant should be baptized. If the parents are Christians, they may want the consolation of having their child claimed as God's own through the sacrament just as they would have if the child survived. This is a point of disagreement among theologians. Some argue that such a baptism is not only meaningless but even denies the true meaning of the sacrament. I see it differently. Christians have long thought of the church as existing in two parts: the church on earth—sometimes called the church militant—and the church in heaven made up of Christians who have died—sometimes called the church triumphant. If we really believe this, why can we not view the baptism of a dying child as incorporation into the church just as we would that of a living child? It is reception into the heavenly church, the communion of saints.

There are also persons who have little interest or commitment to the church who fervently desire immediate baptism for their dying infant. Too often, unfortunately, this desire is driven by superstitious fear. Even so, I believe that pastors should not refuse the sacrament. The crib side of a deathly ill baby is no place for a theological lesson. Pastors should do whatever best evidences the love of God for the child and the family. If there is opportunity for continued ministry with the family later, then that is a wonderful outcome. I am much less in favor of baptisms performed by doctors, nurses, or other hospital personnel unless the family involved is Roman Catholic. The sacraments are God's gift to the church; baptism initiates one into the church. Medical personnel do not represent the church; that is the role of ordained clergy. Baptism by nurses, for example, only encourages the idea that God will not accept the child unless the proper ceremony is performed.

How do you feel about the practice of baptizing dying babies? Why?

What About the Water?

Water was chosen by God as the natural, material element of baptism. It should be used in ways and amounts that manifest its wealth of meanings. The Prayer Over the Water in Section 10 of the liturgy includes many examples. The sound and appearance of water being poured into the font focus attention on its importance. The symbolism of water is made clearest when fonts are of substantial size and are located where the congregation can see them even when no sacrament is being received.

I mentioned earlier the vehement arguments between Methodists along with Presbyterians and Baptists along with Campbellites about infant baptism. These disputes were a prominent feature of the competition between religious groups in our past. The question of an acceptable mode of baptism was just as bitterly debated. Baptists contended that nothing less than total immersion of the body under water was valid. This was, and sometimes still is, another reason that they would not recognize Methodist baptism by sprinkling as the real thing.

Methodists have not been so concerned about either the amount of water nor how it is applied. Throughout our history, Methodism has always allowed a choice of mode by the parents of children being baptized and by adult candidates—sprinkling, pouring, or immersion. We believe that all three modes have likely been used since New Testament times and that each has its own particular symbolism. Sprinkling is the most common mode in our churches, perhaps because it is the simplest. Some pastors use a pitcher of water and pour it over the person's head. Immersion is used less than in the past because so few of our churches have facilities for it. There is some indication of a trend to more buildings with baptisteries and to more use of rivers and lakes. Some churches have fonts large enough to allow babies to be dipped. Any of these modes can be used with persons of any age.

What ideas or feelings do you associate with water? How do these ideas relate to baptism?

Which mode of baptism do you prefer? Can you explain why? Are there different meanings, or at least emphases, in the different modes?

What About Re-baptism?

The sacrament of baptism cannot be repeated. Baptism is an act of God; and once God has done it, it is done! We do not need to give God another chance, and we should not act as if we do not believe that God did it right the first time. People who believe they want to be re-baptized actually need reaffirmation instead. Our relationship with God is like our relationships with other loved ones in our lives. It is dynamic and changing, better some times than at others, even possibly broken and in need of repair at times. Once we have been claimed by God's love and initiated into the body of Christ, God never fails to remain faithful to the divine side of the covenant. It is only the human side of the covenant relationship that can be neglected, even violated, so it is only the human side that needs to be redone.

Our lifelong journey of faith is not a steadily ascending march to spiritual heights, not an unbroken growth in holiness and closeness to God. In reality, it is a back-and-forth, up-and-down process. We need repeated opportunities to recommit ourselves to Christ and renew our pledges of faithful discipleship. Confirmation is the first occasion of affirming our faith. It should be followed by other occasions for reaffirmation. Sometimes we may stray so far from God that we feel that we are lost and that our relationship with God is broken. If so, our God of the baptismal covenant is faithful, ever ready to receive us when we return.

On a blank sheet of paper, draw a line tracing your salvation journey. Is your line straight and ever ascending, or are there peaks and valleys? Can you identify some of those?

SUGGESTIONS FOR THE GROUP SESSION

Gather Supplies

Several copies of *The United Methodist Hymnal* and *The Faith We Sing*; Bibles, large pieces of paper or poster paper and pens; pitcher of water and a bowl; other research resources such as *Word and Table*; *By Water and the Spirit: A United Methodist Understanding of Baptism*; *This Holy Mystery: A United Methodist Understanding of Holy Communion*; *The Interpreter's Dictionary of the Bible*; *The United Methodist Book of Worship*; *The Book of Discipline of The United Methodist Church, 2004*; *The Book of Resolutions of the United Methodist Church, 2004*; and *The Oxford Dictionary of the Christian Church.*

Arrange the Learning Area

- Ahead of time, write the following phrases on a large sheet of paper, one to a sheet, and post them on a wall or other easily visible location.
  "Believer's Baptism"
  "Infant Baptism"
  "Emergency Baptism"
  "Water"
  "Re-baptism"
- Make sure everyone has a place to sit. Arrange the learning area to make group discussion easier.

Lead the Session

- Pour water from a pitcher into a bowl. Invite group members to listen to the water. After a moment of silence, pray together for any needs in the group and for God's guidance as you explore issues and questions related to baptism.
- Ask group members to write on a large piece of paper any questions they have about the phrases.
- Read each of the sections in the chapter using the questions at the end to stimulate discussion. Use the lists made by the group members to stimulate further discussion for each of the sections.
- Celebrate the Congregational Reaffirmation of the Baptismal Covenant on pages 50-53 in the *Hymnal.*
- Sing or read "Baptized in Water" (*The Faith We Sing*, 2248).
- Close the session with a prayer offering thanks to God for the gift of baptism and for the opportunity to nurture one another in life and faith.

Chapter 4

Celebrating Holy Communion

*Come, sinners, to the gospel feast, let every
soul be Jesus' guest.
Ye need not one be left behind, for God hath
bid all humankind.*

*Come and partake the gospel feast, be saved
from sin, in Jesus rest;
O taste the goodness of our God, and eat his
flesh and drink his blood.*

*Ye who believe his record true shall sup with
him and he with you;
come to the feast, be saved from sin, for
Jesus waits to take you in.*[1]

THE SACRAMENT OF HOLY COMMUNION, ALSO
called "Eucharist" and "The Lord's Supper" in most
Protestant traditions, provides spiritual nourishment for a
life of faith. The words *Holy Communion, Eucharist,* and
Lord's Supper carry emphases on particular views of the spiritual nourishment provided in the ritual celebration. Holy
Communion focuses on the holiness of the gathering and

sharing as the body of Christ. Eucharist, from the Greek word for "gratitude," emphasizes giving thanks as Jesus gave thanks for the bread and wine with his disciples at the Last Supper (Luke 22:17-19). The term *the Lord's Supper* was used by Paul (1 Corinthians 11:20) and refers to the Last Supper as he recalled it (1 Corinthians 11:20:23-26).

Roman Catholic Flannery O'Connor is one of my favorite writers. In his novel *The Violent Bear It Away*, O'Connor focuses on a teenager named Tarwater who had grown up living in the woods with his fanatically religious great-uncle who believed himself to be a prophet. After his great-uncle's sudden death, the boy comes into town and lives with his only other relative, his uncle, Rayber. The two are unable to communicate; and, although Rayber tries, he cannot seem to offer the boy what he needs. A particular problem is food. Tarwater absolutely refuses to eat the food that Rayber cooks at home or that is served in restaurants they visit. Late one night, the uncle hears the boy get up and slip out of the house. Rayber follows him, hoping to get a hint of what might appeal to the boy.

> Tarwater's face was strangely lit from the window he was standing before. Rayber watched curiously for a few minutes. It looked to him like the face of someone starving who sees a meal he can't reach laid out before him. At last, something he *wants*, he thought, and determined that tomorrow he would return and buy it. Tarwater reached out and touched the glass and then drew his hand back slowly. He hung there as if he could not take his eyes off what it was he wanted.... Abruptly the boy broke away and moved on.
>
> Rayber stepped out of the entrance and made for the window he had left. He stopped with a shock of disappointment. The place was only a bakery. The window was empty except for a loaf of bread pushed to the side that must have been overlooked when the shelf was cleaned for the night. He stared, puzzled, at the empty window for a second before he started after the boy again.[2]

This story of Tarwater and the bread reminds me of the little girl who after receiving the bread at Holy Communion embarrassed her family and amused the congregation by shouting, "I want more! I want more!" It was not simply bread that Tarwater craved; his hunger was profoundly spiritual.

A real and strong desire for meaningful experiences of Holy Communion exists among United Methodists. Indeed, many people feel that they are being denied, even cheated, when the services of the sacrament in their congregations are not conducted in ways that allow them the sense of Christ's presence. People have a distinct feeling that powerful grace is available in the sacrament and that they want and need it. This is true even though the Lord's Supper has not always been the most popular or best attended of the church's worship services.

I believe that the unpopularity of Holy Communion among some of our members has been the result of the somber, heavy, penitential tone of the service. Confessing our sins is one thing, but being dragged down emotionally and spiritually is another. People are not eager to participate in a service that makes them feel worse when they leave than they did when they came. The older rituals used in our denomination were markedly characterized by emphasis on humility, sin, and repentance. The current ritual in *The United Methodist Hymnal*, however, has a different tone. Without ignoring sin and confession, it emphasizes gratitude and joy for what God has done for us. Its mood is one of celebration.

Another problem has been and remains the tendency of some ministers to tack the sacrament onto the end of an otherwise full-length service. It is not meaningfully connected to the rest of the service—just an add-on. This practice makes Holy Communion an appendix, like the overly long tail wagging on the end of a dog. The chief impression that a congregation may receive is that the Eucharist is mostly something that makes the service run uncomfortably long. It disturbs our dinner times, our tee times, our TV schedules, and our afternoon naps. In spite of such practices, William L. McElvaney, retired professor of worship at Perkins School of Theology, has come to a surprising conclusion. McElvaney reports that he conducted an experiment over a period of 12 years in which he asked many groups of Christians, mainly United Methodists, what they would choose if they had to give up either sermons or Holy Communion for the rest of their lives. Consistently, the majority said they would give up sermons and keep the sacrament.[3]

I am convinced through my experiences with many United Methodists that Holy Communion can, should, and will be desired, even demanded, by our people frequently. I am confident that the sacrament can become a powerful experience of encounter with God, surpassing anything else we do in Christian worship. For this to happen, at least four things are required. First, Holy Communion must become a central ingredient of our worship in Services of Word and Table. Second, the ritual must lead to rejoicing in the presence and gifts of God to God's people. Third, congregations must be educated as to the richness of meanings the sacrament offers so that they come to the table with expectancy and leave it with deepened commitment. Fourth, pastors must conduct the sacramental service with reverent attitudes, powerful words, and meaningful gestures—all appropriate to the profound significance of the occasion.

How does your congregation celebrate Holy Communion? What feelings or thoughts do you have about Holy Communion? How does Holy Communion affect your commitment to serving Christ?

What's It All About Anyway?

The Services of Word and Table include musical settings for use if the congregational responses are to be sung rather than said. Service I provides text for an entire service of worship, including the Eucharist. Service II contains only the ritual for Holy Communion. The study edition of *This Holy Mystery: A United Methodist Understanding of Holy Communion* will be a helpful resource in this discussion, so the relevant pages will be noted at the end of this chapter.

The term *Word and Table* indicates that a full service of Christian worship includes the proclamation of the Word (in Scripture, preaching, prayer, and song) and the celebration at the Table (Holy Communion).

Holy Communion is important because it is a time when we encounter Jesus Christ. The "Table of the Lord" is precisely that. Christ is present in ways that we cannot explain.[4] In Communion, we do not simply remember what God has done for us in the past; we experience what God is doing here and now. If we could understand this reality of Christ's presence, we might run down the aisles of our churches in our enthusiasm.

John Wesley recognized the immense importance of Holy Communion in the lives of Christian people. He preached on "The Duty of Constant Communion," wrote and published with his brother Charles 166 hymns on the Lord's Supper, and received the sacrament himself as often as possible. Wesley described Holy Communion as "the grand channel whereby the grace of [God's] Spirit was conveyed to the souls of all the children of God."[5] What did he mean by this grace that is conveyed to us in Holy Communion?

Grace means "the free, undeserved favor and love of God."[6] Grace given in Holy Communion can be examined in terms of the spiritual benefits received. First, Holy Communion is a place of forgiveness. Early in the ritual, we confess our individual and corporate sins and receive God's forgiveness as announced by the presiding pastor. Wesley said, "The grace of God given herein confirms to us the pardon of our sins by enabling us to leave them."[7]

Second, Holy Communion provides us the nourishment we need for the journey of salvation. Just as food and drink are essential to maintain our physical bodies, so our spiritual lives need to be sustained continually and strengthened by divine grace. Wesley said of the Lord's Supper, "This is the food of our souls: this gives strength to perform our duty, and leads us on to perfection."[8]

Third, receiving Holy Communion is transformative. It puts us in touch with the power of God to make us into the people God wants us to be. The sacrament is sometimes described as "converting." This does not usually refer to a person's first experience of conversion but to the ongoing converting or changing through which our relationship with Christ is deepened. We surrender more and more of ourselves to God and are progressively shaped into the image of Christ.

Fourth, Eucharist is a time for healing, especially for reconciliation between God and us and between others and us. We do not dine privately; we eat and drink together with God's people and realize that we are bound to all those with whom we share the meal. This reconciliation is not limited to a local congregation but should extend to all persons, societies, and nations with whom we are not at peace.

Fifth, Holy Communion prepares us for and propels us into mission. The grace that we have received is to be used in work in the world toward conditions of justice and peace. We are charged to continue Christ's work of redeeming the world.

In summary, we might say that Holy Communion is our lifeline. A deep-sea diver depends for his very life on the constant supply of air from above him. As Christians, we must have a constant supply of divine presence, love, and power if we are to live in faith. The sacrament is the lifeline through which these flow to us.

How do you respond to the following statement from the above section? "In Communion, we do not simply remember what God has done for us in the past; we experience what God is doing here and now." How might our experience of the sacrament be changed by taking it seriously?

How do you respond to John Wesley's comment, "This is the food of our souls: This gives strength to perform our duty, and leads us on to perfection"? Do you experience Holy Communion like this? What might help you to do so?

Our Liturgy for Holy Communion

The words of our Holy Communion ritual contain all the meanings I have mentioned and more. Let us look carefully at the ritual in the hope of deepening our understanding and appreciation. I will begin with a look at the Service for Word and Table II.[9]

The ritual of Holy Communion begins with the Invitation: "Christ our Lord invites to his table all who love him, / who earnestly repent of their sin / and seek to live in peace with one another."[10] The Invitation is an essential part of the ritual because it makes clear who is being invited to the table. There are appropriate attitudes and desires that persons should at least want to have when they come to dine with Christ. The invitation is open, but it is not causal. Receiving Holy Communion implies an openness to the Spirit, a desire for something that Christ offers. I do not mean to place requirements or limits that might discourage persons from communing but simply to indicate how we come so as to be most receptive to God's grace. Love for Christ is more than a feeling; it is a willingness to live as he would have us to. In order to repent of our sin, we need to be aware of it.

The Confession and Pardon is important because we need to deal with our sin before we approach the table. Note that the word is *sin*, not *sins*. Sin is a condition of brokenness in our relationship to God; it is a falling short of what God wills for us. To repent means to turn around and to go in another direction. We come to the Lord's Table recognizing our sin and wishing to change. "Therefore, let us confess our sin before God and one another."[11] Confession expresses our awareness of sin and our regret. Notice that this is not a private confession but one that we share with the gathered congregation. Here, as throughout the service, we see that Holy Communion is a celebration of the whole community, not an act of personal piety. We commune with one another as well as with Christ.[12]

We recognize that we have sinned because "we have not loved you with our whole heart."[13] This may be the sin of individuals, but it is also the sin of the corporate community: "We have failed to be an obedient church. / We have not done your will, / we have broken your law, / we have rebelled against your love."[14] These are sins of action or of failure to act. They are violations of our responsibility to other people. "We have not loved our neighbors, / and we have not heard the cry of the needy."[15] Having confessed these sins, we ask God to "forgive us, we pray. / Free us for joyful obedience, / through Jesus Christ our Lord."[16] In addressing God, an old English prayer says, "O God, who art the author of peace and lover of concord, . . . whose service is perfect freedom."[17] This is the kind of freedom we seek—freedom from what separates us from God and other people.

Amen, here and throughout the ritual, is our affirmation, meaning, "So be it!" A period of silent prayer provides the opportunity for reflection on our sin and desire for forgiveness. Then, the presiding pastor makes the joyous announcement: "Hear the good news: / Christ died for us while we were yet sinners; / that proves God's love toward us. / In the name of Jesus Christ, you are forgiven!"[18] In turn, the congregation responds, "In the name of Jesus Christ, you are forgiven."[19] It is God who forgives, but we proclaim this forgiveness to one another. The presiding pastor has no special authority to forgive sin. We believe in what is often called "the priesthood of all believers": Clergy announces forgiveness to the congregation and the congregation to the clergy. Then, together, we praise God: "Glory to God. Amen."[20]

Peace with God is followed by the healing of relationships with one another. Because we have received forgiveness, we are able to "offer one another signs of reconciliation and love."[21] The barriers between us and other people have been broken down by God's forgiveness of us all, and we express this in words and actions. The Peace is more than a time of greeting—a time for "Good Morning," "How are you?" or "Glad to see you." It is an act of reconciliation and blessing. Appropriate words are "May the peace of Christ be with you" or "God bless you." The Peace that we are sharing comes from Christ, not from us. I am aware that some people are uncomfortable with the Peace. It is an ancient gesture of love within the community of faith; indeed, there are five references in the New Testament to the holy kiss or the kiss of love. Appropriate actions include handshakes or hugs for those standing around us or others whom we can reach in the congregation. Moving around is fine. These gestures should authentically express the intimacy between people in the congregation and should not be forced or faked.

How does your congregation practice "passing the peace"? How do people feel about it? Would it enrich the practice if people understood better what it means?

Next, is the time for the Offering, because it is "as forgiven and reconciled people"[22] that we can "offer ourselves and our gifts to God."[23] Monetary gifts are collected and presented at the chancel. A meaningful practice is to have the elements of bread and wine brought forward and given to the presiding pastor. This action communicates that the wheat and the grapes of God's creation have been made by human beings into the elements we use. What God has given, we give back for God's use. Anyone may bring the bread and wine forward: ushers, perhaps the person who baked the loaf, sometimes children.

Holy Communion includes four actions by the presiding pastor and the congregation that echo the actions of Jesus in the upper room in his last supper with the disciples. The first is Taking the Bread and Cup. The pastor takes the bread and cup, which have been brought forward; or, if they are already on the table, the pastor removes any lids or coverings to prepare for the meal.

The Great Thanksgiving prayer is the heart of the celebration of Holy Communion.[24] It is led by an authorized representative of the church—an ordained elder or another person who is appointed to be in charge of a congregation. The words are a prayer of the whole gathered people who participate by their responses. The prayer, which blesses the bread and the wine, is the second act of Holy Communion. The first six lines are an opening dialogue, calling the congregation to encounter with the living Christ. It is appropriate for the presiding pastor to raise his or her arms in the ancient gesture of prayer. The emphasis on thanksgiving reminds us of the meaning of Holy Communion. For a fuller view of the Great Thanksgiving, we turn to the longer version in Service of Word and Table I.[25] There are a variety of Great Thanksgiving prayers that may be used for special occasions and seasons in the church year.[26]

The Great Thanksgiving is a summary of God's mighty acts of salvation as recorded in the Old and New Testaments. God is first praised as "creator of heaven and earth"[27] who "formed us in your image and breathed into us the breath of life."[28] The loving, harmonious relationship with God for which we were created was broken "when we turned away, and our love failed."[29] However, God's "love remained steadfast"[30] and God acted in history: "You delivered us from captivity, made covenant to be our sovereign God, / and spoke to us through your prophets."[31] These words are a brief sketch of the acts of God in the Old Testament.

In response to these divine acts, the congregation says, "And so, with your people on earth and all the company of heaven / we praise your name and join their unending hymn."[32] The idea of the company of heaven praising God unceasingly comes from Isaiah 6:3 and Revelation 4:8-11. The congregational hymn is called the "Sanctus," meaning "holy." The term reflects the acclamation of the crowd when Jesus entered Jerusalem at the beginning of Holy Week (Matthew 21:9): "Holy, holy, holy Lord, God of power and might, / heaven and earth are full of your glory. / Hosanna in the highest. / Blessed is he who comes in the name of the Lord. / Hosanna in the highest."[33] In Hebrew, *hosanna* means "O save" but has became more generally used as a glad expression of praise.

At this point, the Great Thanksgiving moves to God's work of salvation through Jesus Christ: "Holy are you, and blessed is your Son Jesus Christ."[34] The emphasis is on Jesus' ministry of liberating and healing, what we might call social justice. The words recount Jesus' first message in the synagogue in his hometown of Nazareth (Luke 4:16-19) when he spoke from Isaiah: "Your Spirit anointed him / to preach good news to the poor, / to proclaim release to the captives / and recovering of sight to the blind, / to set at liberty those who are oppressed, / and to announce that the time had come / when you would save your people. / He healed the sick, fed the hungry, and ate with sinners."[35]

It was not only Jesus' earthly ministry that made our salvation possible ("By the baptism of his suffering, death, and resurrection / you gave birth to your church, / delivered us from slavery to sin and death, / and made with us a new covenant / by water and the Spirit."[36]); but Jesus spoke of his suffering and death as a baptism (Mark 10:38-40; Luke 12:50), meaning a profound commitment to and an acceptance of God's way. The church is the result of Jesus' death and resurrection, composed of those who accept the freedom from sin that he made possible and enter into covenant relationship with God. Our baptism, by water and the Spirit (John 3:5), makes us members of that community of the new covenant (Luke 22:20; 1 Corinthians 11:25). Jesus' presence with his disciples did not end when he was no longer with them in the flesh. That same presence is promised to us: "When the Lord Jesus ascended, / he promised to be with us always, / in the power of your Word and Holy Spirit."[37]

How do you respond to the list of the various events in the history of salvation that the Great Thanksgiving asks us to recall? Which has most meaning for you? Why?

The next part of the Great Thanksgiving is called the "institution narrative" because it tells the story of Jesus' instituting or beginning the Lord's Supper (1 Corinthians 11:23-26): "On the night in which he gave himself up for us, / he took bread, gave thanks to you, broke the bread, / gave it to his disciples."[38] These are the four basic actions of the Eucharist. "And said: / 'Take, eat; this is my body which is given for you. / Do this in remembrance of me.' / When the supper was over, / he took the cup, / gave thanks to you, gave it to his disciples, and said: / 'Drink from this, all of you; / this is my blood of the new covenant, / poured out for you and for many / for the forgiveness of sins. / Do this, as often as you drink it, / in remembrance of me.' "[39] By giving the bread to his disciples, Jesus signified that his body broken on the cross would make possible our salvation.

In the Old Testament, covenants between humans and God were almost always sealed or marked with blood. Circumcision, the sign of the covenant between God and the people of Israel, involves blood. Jesus' blood sealed the new covenant between God and the Christian church. We are repeatedly to receive Christ's body and blood for the forgiveness of our sins and in memory of Jesus' sacrifice. United Methodists understand this language to be figurative: The bread and the wine represent the body and the blood of Christ but do not become them.

The emphasis on remembrance here has been made visible to many of us by the words *in remembrance of me*, which are carved on the front of Communion tables. We must never forget what Christ has done as well as what he is doing and what he will do. Because we remember what God has done for us in Christ, "we offer ourselves in praise and thanksgiving / as a holy and living sacrifice, / in union with Christ's offering for us, / as we proclaim the mystery of faith."[40]

In order for God's gracious actions on our behalf to be beneficial, we must respond by accepting them in faith. We are to join with Christ in offering ourselves, surrendering ourselves to God, and being consecrated for service (Romans 12:1). Much of faith is a mystery, far beyond our complete comprehension in this life; but we believe and affirm together that "Christ has died; Christ is risen; Christ will come again."[41]

The latter portion of the Great Thanksgiving is an invocation, or calling, for the presence and action of the Holy Spirit (an *epiclesis* in Greek). With appropriate gestures to the congregation and over the elements, the presiding pastor prays, "Pour out your Holy Spirit on us gathered here, and on these gifts of bread and wine."[42] We believe that the Holy Spirit, the presence of Christ, does come and is active in Holy Communion. The Spirit is asked to "make them [the bread and wine] be for us the body and blood of Christ, / that we may be for the world the body of Christ, / redeemed by his blood."[43] No change in the elements themselves is implied here. The change is in their power to transform us. The church is to go out into the world doing what Christ did, giving as Christ gave, continuing the work of redeeming the world.

The Spirit also exercises the power to make the Holy Communion experience "communion": "By your Spirit make us one with Christ, / one with each other, / and one in ministry to all the world."[44] Holy Communion is a foretaste of our future with God: "Until Christ comes in final victory and we feast at his heavenly banquet."[45] The Bible speaks several times about the great banquet in heaven with Christ where we will celebrate being with him forever. Jesus told the disciples that he would not drink "this fruit of the vine until that day when I drink it new with you in my Father's kingdom" (Matthew 26:29; see also Luke 14:15; 22:18, 30; Revelation 19:9). We believe that God, who created the world, will bring the age to an end in God's own way and time. Evil and sin will eventually be destroyed, and peace and justice will prevail.

The section ends with a doxology: "Through your Son Jesus Christ, / with the Holy Spirit in your holy church, / all honor and glory is yours, almighty Father, / now and forever."[46] The congregation claims the Great Thanksgiving prayer as its own with the concluding amen.

Having celebrated the relationship with God that we enjoy, as individuals and as the church, we can pray "with the confidence of children of God. Since the sixth century, Christians have prayed this prayer immediately after the

Great Thanksgiving. The version of the Lord's Prayer in the ritual is an ecumenical translation, but a more familiar version may be used.

The third act of Holy Communion is Breaking the Bread. This is best done using a whole loaf that is lifted and torn apart in view of the congregation. The optional words "because there is one loaf, / we, who are many, are one body, for we all partake of the one loaf"[47] refer to 1 Corinthians 10:17 and stress the unity of the church. The chalice or cup should be lifted into view. First Corinthians 10:16 is the source of the words: "The bread which we break is a sharing in the body of Christ. / The cup over which we give thanks is a sharing in the blood of Christ."[48] The emphasis is on sharing and oneness with Christ and with one another. Note that there is no "magic moment" in the ritual when the occasion is infused with spiritual power. We believe that God is at work in and throughout the service.[49]

The fourth act is Giving the Bread and Cup. Appropriate words to accompany these actions are "The body of Christ, given for you. / The blood of Christ, given for you."[50] The person receiving responds, "Amen."[51] Other phrases such as "The body of Christ, the bread of life. The blood of Christ, the cup of salvation" may also be used.

Receiving the bread and cup by all present who wish to do so is followed by a prayer: "Eternal God, we give you thanks for this holy mystery / in which you have given yourself for us."[52] This sentence is, of course, the source of the name of United Methodism's official document on Holy Communion, *This Holy Mystery: A United Methodist Understanding of Holy Communion.*

"Grant that we may go into the world / in the strength of your Spirit, / to give ourselves for others, / in the name of Jesus Christ our Lord. / Amen."[53] The grace that we receive in Holy Communion is to be put into practice through our work in the world for others.[54] The service ends with a traditional American Methodist benediction or blessing that may also be used on other occasions.

There are a multitude of meanings that appear in the ritual; and what we hear may vary from time to time, according to our own experiences or needs. It is, however, striking how thoroughly at least seven themes of meaning are interwoven throughout the ritual: communion or togetherness, thanksgiving, real presence of Christ, forgiveness, remembrance, foreshadowing of eternity, and ministry or service.

Examine the ritual for Holy Communion, and locate places where the themes of communion or togetherness, thanksgiving, real presence of Christ, forgiveness, remembrance, foreshadowing of eternity, and ministry or service appear. Which ones mean the most to you? Why? How might the others enrich your life of faith?

SUGGESTIONS FOR THE GROUP SESSION

Gather Supplies

Several copies of *The United Methodist Hymnal* and *The Faith We Sing*; Bibles; large sheets of paper or poster paper and pens; *By Water and the Spirit: A United Methodist Understanding of Baptism*; *This Holy Mystery: A United Methodist Understanding of Holy Communion*; *The Interpreter's Dictionary of the Bible*; *The United Methodist Book of Worship*; *The Book of Discipline of The United Methodist Church, 2004*; *The Book of Resolutions of The United Methodist Church, 2004*; and *The Oxford Dictionary of the Christian Church*.

Arrange the Learning Area

• Ahead of time write each of the following words on a large sheet of paper, one to a sheet, and post them on a wall or another easily visible location.

"Holy Communion"
"Eucharist"
"The Lord's Supper"
- Make sure everyone has a place to sit. Arrange the learning area to facilitate group discussion.

Lead the Session

- Open the session with a prayer for any needs in the group and for God's guidance as you explore the ritual of Holy Communion and consider ways it helps people experience the nurturing grace of God in Jesus Christ.
- Ask group members to write on a large sheet of paper any questions they have about the words *Holy Communion, Eucharist,* and *The Lord's Supper.*
- Read each of the sections in the chapter using the questions in these sections to stimulate discussion. Use the lists the group created earlier to stimulate further discussion for each of the sections.
- Sing or read the hymn "Come Sinners to the Gospel Feast" (*Hymnal,* 616).
- Close the session with a prayer offering thanks to God for the gift of Holy Communion and for the empowering presence of Christ.

Chapter 5

Questions About Holy Communion

O the depths of love divine, the unfath-
omable grace!
Who shall say how bread and wine God into
us conveys!
How the bread his flesh imparts, how the
wine transmits his blood,
Fills his faithful people's hearts with all the
life of God.[1]

A S WITH BAPTISM, CONSIDERATION OF HOLY
Communion uncovers a variety of questions, opinions, and
emotions. The Wesley hymn above makes clear that we can
never really understand the mystery of the sacrament.
However, let us examine several issues in an effort to deepen
our understanding and to enhance our practice.

How Often Should We Celebrate Holy Communion?

John Wesley answered this question when he said, "It is
the duty of every Christian to receive the Lord's Supper as
often as he can.... Because the benefits of doing it are so
great to all that do it in obedience to him; namely, the forgiveness of our past sins and the present strengthening and

refreshing of our souls."[2] I feel confident that if we were as certain of the benefits of Holy Communion as Wesley was, we would demand that the sacrament be served in our churches frequently.

In the early Christian church, Holy Communion was observed every Sunday. This practice has continued in most Christian traditions. However, during the 18th and 19th centuries in America, the custom of quarterly communion developed. In some congregations, this schedule is still so ingrained that one might think it is written somewhere in the Bible: "Thou shall not commune more than once a quarter." In reality, the quarterly sacrament was the most that was available because of the lack of ordained preachers, especially in the rural areas and small settlements. The presiding elder (district superintendent) was only able to get to every preaching place every three months. Those joyous occasions were called quarterly meetings. They included business, worship, baptisms, and Holy Communion. The rest of the time, worship was led by a layperson who was not authorized to administer the sacraments. Methodist practice, following Wesley, was and is to limit sacramental responsibility to ordained elders. Since 1972, the church has allowed exceptions to this rule in order to make the sacraments more readily available. A commissioned or licensed minister is able to offer baptism and the Lord's Supper in the church or charge to which he or she is appointed. This exception, plus a larger percentage of ordained elders and easier transportation between churches, means that an authorized person can be present every Sunday in most congregations.

For the last several decades, celebrations of Holy Communion have been increasing in frequency. The most common pattern today appears to be monthly, often on the first Sunday of the month. The recommendation in *This Holy Mystery: A United Methodist Understanding of Holy*

Communion is "congregations of The United Methodist Church are encouraged to move toward a richer sacramental life, including weekly celebration of the Lord's Supper at the services on the Lord's Day."[3] If this weekly celebration is to be appropriately significant, it will require serious dealing with issues of worship planning, use of time, integration of Word and Table, and exploring the multiple richness of meanings of the sacrament.

How often does your church celebrate Holy Communion? Would you like to see it done more often? Why or why not?

Who Is Invited?

United Methodist churches offer what is called an "open table." This means that there are few, if any, requirements that a person must meet in order to receive. This practice differs from that of most other Christian churches. We believe that the table belongs to Christ, not to us, and that Christ's welcome is wide. God works through the Eucharist in many ways, offering to every person the grace that is needed at their point on the journey of salvation. The sacrament might provide the first opportunity for a person to recognize their sin and ask for forgiveness. It might give strength and nourishment for ongoing progress in Christian living. It might be the occasion when someone is so filled with divine love that nothing else matters.

The New Testament records numerous occasions when Jesus ate with people who did not fulfill the requirements that society thought essential to being a good person. Indeed, Jesus seemed to go out of his way to share meals with the disreputable and to admonish those who believed themselves righteous. He taught about a great feast that was declined by those who were invited and enjoyed by guests who were gathered in from the streets and byways. The table fellowship of Jesus with all kinds of people is our model as we extend a broad invitation to come and dine with him at the table of Holy Communion. Because God's grace is free and abundant, the church offers Holy Communion with generosity rather than stinginess or exclusivity.

This generosity does not mean that persons are invited to the table casually. It should be made clear in the invitation that while no barriers are erected, coming to participate in the Lord's Supper is a significant act. It implies at least a sense of needing something from God and of opening oneself to receive. Responding to the invitation means accepting the responsibility of allowing divine grace to work on and within one.

Few other denominational traditions practice such an open table. In most, there is at least the prerequisite of having been baptized before receiving Holy Communion. There is no question that the early Christian church admitted only the baptized to share in the holy meal. All others were excused from the service after the proclaiming of the Word and before the sacrament. Even John Wesley, in spite of his preaching about the availability of divine grace to all, imposed certain requirements for admission to Holy Communion. Wesley wanted Methodists to show evidence in their lives that they were living rightly and seeking God. If not, he would not admit them to the table.

American Methodism moved decidedly in the direction of an open table without limitations or restraints. Partly, this was in response to the Baptist practice of refusing to admit any who had not been immersed. Methodist openness became and remains a distinctive mark of our church's practice.

The lack of a baptismal requirement for Holy Communion should not be understood as indicating that baptism is optional or of placing less value on it. Anyone who has not been baptized but who regularly participates in Holy

Communion should be counseled by the pastor. There may be a misunderstanding about the relationship between the sacraments. Baptism and Holy Communion are closely linked. This will be powerfully expressed in the congregation if services of baptism are immediately followed by celebrations of Holy Communion.

What does our practice of an "open table" say about God?

Should We Let the Little Ones Come?

What about the participation of children in Holy Communion? Some congregations and some parents think that children should reach a certain age or that they should be confirmed before participating in the Lord's Supper. This was more common in the past; but now United Methodism affirms that when we say, "All are invited" to the table and that the invitation includes all ages. When infants or children are baptized, they become baptized members of the church and are certainly entitled to participate in the church's other sacrament. Indeed, at the end of the rituals of baptism, including the one designated for infant baptism, the last instruction reads, "It is most fitting that the service continue with Holy Communion, in which the union of the new members with the body of Christ is most fully expressed. The new members may receive first."[4] Eastern Orthodox churches have always communed baptized infants. While they do it with spoons of silver or gold, we use the finger of the pastor dipped into the cup.

Children understand what it is to eat before they know what it is to pray. In fact, the first way that a child experiences nurture and care is in being fed. For them, the connection between being loved and being given food and drink is real. If we leave our children behind in the pew when we go forward to receive the consecrated elements, often with words of warning about good behavior, what message are we sending them?

Children need to know they are part of the community of faith and that they are welcomed by God and the congregation. They should not be taught that the church is only for grownups and that they are outsiders.

The objection is often raised that children do not understand what Holy Communion means. My response is, "Do you understand it?" Of course, we understand more than children do; but in comparison to the profound significance of "this holy mystery," our comprehension, too, is limited and partial. Eating and drinking with Jesus, receiving God's love and care, are not dependent on knowledge in the head but openness in the heart.

How would you explain to a four-year-old what Holy Communion means? to a 12-year-old? to an adult?

Who Is Worthy?

Sometimes there are people in the congregation who will not participate in the Lord's Supper because they believe that they are not worthy. Often this results from a misunderstanding of 1 Corinthians 11:27-32. Such humble, conscientious Christians are in no danger of "eating and drinking to their own damnation." They need to be helped to understand that none of us, by our own efforts, can make ourselves worthy of this great gift. However, thank God, it is not our personal worthiness that matters; it is the worthiness of Christ in which we participate because of his grace. No one is worthy; no one has to be. Indeed, if we were worthy to receive the body and blood of Christ, we would not need to do so.

Examination of our spiritual state before receiving Eucharist is an appropriate thing to do. Recognition of our sinfulness and weakness shows us our need. We come to the table of the Lord because of those needs, because there we can be forgiven and we can receive strength to continue in the journey with Christ.

One of my favorite phrases in the ritual of Holy Communion is "he ate with sinners." How do you respond to this phrase?

How Do We Receive the Consecrated Elements?

There is no one correct way of distributing and receiving the bread and the wine. Following traditional practice in the American past, many congregations come forward in groups and kneel at the communion rail. Kneeling is a sign of respect, even reverence. Some congregations pass plates of the elements along the pews and partake seated. Increasingly, people are coming forward and receiving while standing. This posture can be understood as a sign of the resurrection of Christ.

In any of these modes, the bread can be given by the server, passed from person to person, or taken as precut pieces or wafers from a plate. The wine can be in individual cups in a tray held by the server or passed from person to person. More and more congregations are using intinction, a mode in which the piece of bread is dipped into the cup of wine and then eaten.

All these practices have their advantages and disadvantages. Kneeling at the rail is meaningful but also a slow way of communing a large congregation. Passing the plates along the rows is less meaningful to me because it does not require the people to do anything. Receiving at the rail while standing is good but should always be accompanied by a clear invitation to kneel in prayer either before or after receiving. I believe that the bread should be placed by the server into the communicant's cupped hands—grace is neither grabbed nor self-served.

The use of a whole loaf of bread that is broken and served in generous portions is best. It is difficult to be reminded of the abundance of divine grace when one is being offered a thin wafer or a fish-food size piece of bread. The use of a single chalice or cup from which the people either drink or into which the bread is dipped is best. Individual "shot glasses" provide little sense of sharing and togetherness. If they must be used, they can be filled at the table from a pitcher or pouring chalice. The single loaf and cup express the unity of the body of Christ, the gathered community at one with one another and with Christ.

How does your congregation distribute and receive the consecrated elements? Would you be open to other modes? Why or why not?

What About Germs?

Decisions about what methods to use in distributing and receiving elements are often influenced by concerns about hygiene and fear of communicable diseases. These are serious matters and must be dealt with realistically. Certainly, pastors and others who are serving should wash their hands before touching the elements. This is often done simply with a bowl of water placed on the table, but much more effective is the use of hand sanitizer. A small bottle can be used without too much display and will help to reassure the congregation.

It is more sanitary for one server to distribute the bread than for people to serve themselves. If individual cups are used, they should be handed out by the server, since it is virtually impossible to remove a single cup without touching others. The use of a single large cup or chalice for dipping is hygienic if pieces of bread are large enough for dipping without touching the cup or liquid.

What About the Bread and the Wine?

Any kind of bread, leavened or unleavened, is acceptable. If you are fortunate enough to have someone in your congregation who will bake loaves, that is wonderful. Except in special circumstances, an uncut loaf is best. It is a much stronger symbol than wafers or precut pieces. If there are persons in the congregation who are gluten-intolerant or who have similar problems, provision should be made to offer bread that meets their needs.

Throughout this book, I refer to the drink in Holy Communion as wine, although I am aware that most United Methodist churches serve grape juice. I do this because the historic practice of the Christian church and the practice of most of Christianity today involve using wine. Even in the ritual, we speak of "wine." Somehow "bread and juice" sounds much less significant. Methodists used wine in the Lord's Supper until the temperance and prohibition movements of the late 19th and early 20th century raised moral questions about alcoholic beverages. The development of pasteurization of grape juice by the Thomas Welch family at about the same time made an alcohol-free alternative available.

Today there is no absolute prohibition on the use of wine in Holy Communion.[5] Some churches are serving it in order to reclaim traditional and ecumenical Christian practice. As dialogues with the Episcopal and Lutheran churches continue toward harmonizing our practices, this trend is likely to accelerate. It is important that an alcohol-free option be provided for those for whom medical issues or moral scruples are a problem.

What difference does it make in the celebration of Holy Communion if a single loaf is broken and served? if a single cup or chalice is used? if grape juice or wine is served?

What Should Be Done With the Leftovers?

Just as we sometimes have leftovers after our meals at home, there may be leftovers after Communion. Often there are more consecrated elements than are needed to serve everyone present The most significant use of this bread and wine is to take it to those who are unable to be at the worship service. Members of the congregation who are shut-in, ill, working, or in institutions need to be included in the celebration of Holy Communion. Using the consecrated elements, laypersons can lead a brief ritual and serve these people wherever they are. This should be done as soon as possible after the sacrament is celebrated by the congregation.

The pastor, servers, and members of the congregation, including children, can appropriately consume the elements at the end of the service. Elements still remaining should be disposed of in ways that honor their use for a holy purpose. They may be poured upon the ground and scattered to the birds, buried, or burned. Consecrated elements should not be returned to their containers for future use.

Does your church take consecrated elements to persons who are unable to attend? Would you be willing to do this? What kind of preparation and training would you need?

SUGGESTIONS FOR THE GROUP SESSION

Gather Supplies

Several copies of *The United Methodist Hymnal* and *The Faith We Sing*; Bibles; large sheets of paper or poster paper and pens; *By Water and the Spirit: A United Methodist Understanding of Baptism*; *This Holy Mystery: A United Methodist Understanding of Holy Communion*; *The Interpreter's Dictionary of the Bible*; *The United Methodist Book of Worship*; *The Book of Discipline of The United Methodist Church, 2004*; *The Book of Resolutions of The United Methodist Church, 2004*; and *The Oxford Dictionary of the Christian Church.*

Make arrangements with your pastor ahead of time to celebrate Holy Communion with your group.

Arrange the Learning Area

• Ahead of time, prepare a worship center. Find a small table. Cover it with an attractive tablecloth or a piece of fabric. Place a candle in a candleholder and the elements for Holy Communion on the worship center. Light the candle.
• Make sure everyone has a place to sit. Arrange the learning area to facilitate group discussion.

Lead the Session

• Pray together for God's guidance as you explore issues and questions related to Holy Communion.
• Read each of the sections in the chapter, using the questions in the sections to stimulate discussion.

- With your pastor officiating, celebrate Holy Communion, using A Service of Word and Table II (*Hymnal*, pages 12-15).
- Sing or read the hymn "O the Depth of Love Divine" (*Hymnal*, 627).
- Close the session with a prayer offering thanks to God for the gift of Holy Communion and for the strength to serve Christ and one another in life and faith.

Chapter 6

Living as Baptized and Communing Christians

Baptized into thy name, Mysterious One in Three,
Our souls and bodies claim, sacrifice to thee:
We only live our faith to prove, the faith which works by humble love.

O that our light may shine, and all our lives express
The character divine, the real holiness![1]

Now let us from this table rise renewed in body, mind, and soul;
with Christ we die and live again, his self-less love has made us whole.[2]

So WHAT? WHAT DIFFERENCE DOES BAPTISM AND Holy Communion make in our lives? The "so what" question is always important. I think it should be asked at the end of every sermon preached and every lesson taught. Certainly it should be asked at the conclusion of this study of the sacraments in United Methodism. How are we to live as baptized and communing Christians?

How do you respond to the question, "How are we to live as baptized and communing Christians?"

Shaped by Sacraments Into Sacrament

As the body of Christ, the church is to be sacramental in the world. In other words, the church is to be the physical vehicle through which divine grace is conveyed to human beings. The church is shaped for this task by the grace of God working through baptism and Eucharist. Our sacraments offer us "grace unto," grace that is not just an end in itself but a means to a greater end. Sacramental grace forms and empowers us for ministry in the world.

In baptism and Holy Communion, we experience God's giving of the divine Self to us in love. We respond by giving ourselves to God and to God's work on the earth. We are enabled to love our neighbors in ways that make God's love visible and concrete. This love is expressed in efforts to build a more just and peaceful society. Having received so generously from God, we are motivated to "go into the world / in the strength of [his] Spirit / to give ourselves for others."[3]

However, not only is the church to work for a peaceful and just society, it is to *be* such a society, a model and an inspiration for the world. Of course, the church will never be perfect, for it is composed of imperfect persons; but it should be different. The kinds of selfishness, discrimination, and inequality that characterize the secular society have no place in the community of faith. If the promises of God are true, the church must fulfill them. If the commandments of God are real, the church must keep them. In so doing, the church will show to the world an example of life lived as intended by God who created us.

Probably you have heard the old proverb: "What you do speaks so loudly, I cannot hear what you say." The world will never believe the Christian message unless it sees that good news lived out by a community of faithful people who have been shaped by grace into a community of love and forgiveness, acceptance and inclusion, justice and peace.

How do you understand the significance of the church as sacramental to the world? What are some specific ways that the church can function as a sacramental community in our world?

Baptism: The Sacrament of Radical Equality

In 1667, the legislature of the colony of Virginia passed a law making it clear that the baptism of a slave did not mean that the slave was to be free.[4] The fact that such a law was thought to be necessary indicates that the American colonists were struggling with the relationship of baptism to freedom and equality. Clearly there were those who felt that a person who had become one's brother or sister in Christ through baptism should not also be anyone's slave. The apostle Paul recognized this radical equality of all baptized persons in Galatians 3:27-28: "As many of you as were baptized into Christ have clothed yourselves with Christ. There is no longer Jew or Greek, there is no longer slave or free, there is no longer male or female; for all of you are one in Christ Jesus."

The theology of Methodism insists that all persons are in need of divine grace and that all persons are offered that grace. God's grace is made available to us freely and completely without any achievement of our own. This even-handed, open-handedness of God tells us emphatically that everyone is equally valued by God and should be so valued by us. All human pretensions of rank or merit are simply false—worse, they are sinful. We come to the baptismal font in equal need of grace; each of us is as undeserving as the others. We are restored to right relationship with God and, thus, to right relationship with one another. If we are God's children, we must recognize others as our sisters and brothers, a family without favorites and free from sibling rivalries.

How would life in our congregations change if we understood ourselves as sisters and brothers in Christ and free from sibling rivalry?

Holy Communion: The Sacrament Of Radical Justice

Jim Wallis, of *Sojourners* magazine, tells the story of an old table in an Anglican church in London. Years ago, it was used by William Wilberforce, the great English crusader against slavery, to write his letters to the British Parliament appealing for the abolition of human bondage throughout the empire. The table is now used as the table of the Lord when Holy Communion is served in that church.[5]

There is a profound connection between the Eucharist and justice for all of God's people. When Paul was trying to teach the Corinthian church the real meaning of the Lord's Supper, he instructed them, "So then, my brothers and sisters, when you come together to eat, wait for one another" (1 Corinthians 11:33).

Could it be that we are to wait to enjoy the good things of the world until others have access to them as well? We come to the table as we come to the font: in common need of God's love, forgiveness, and strengthening. At the table, we are reminded of the injustice that causes some of us to have so much and others to have so little. What God has given freely, we distribute and use unfairly. At the table, we share the good things that God has created as we are to share them in the world—so that all have enough.

In what ways is radical justice revealed to you as you commune at Christ's table?

Is Your Church a Model?

One of the roles of the church is to serve as a model of an equalitarian, just, and peaceful community. It is to be a community living in accord with Christ's commandment to love one another. Baptism and Holy Communion show us the vision and challenge and empower us to fulfill it. The church must examine itself. If there is conflict, injustice, and discrimination within, the church cannot offer the pattern of community that the world needs.

List the ways in which you think your church is and is not a model for the world as God intends it to be. What changes are necessary for your church to become such a model? How can it be accomplished?

Social Religion and Social Holiness

John Wesley insisted that true religion involved faith in Christ and growth in holiness of life. Such holiness was not only individual and pietistic but social and activist. Wesley taught that there is "no religion but social religion, no holiness but social holiness."[6] The Christian life is to be one of service to one's fellow human beings, avoiding harm and doing good. Wesley worked for the alleviation of human suffering and for transformation of the corrupt social order that caused suffering.

The sacraments have to do not only with our personal relationship to God in Christ but also with our relationship to other people. The font and table bring all human institutions under the divine judgment. The Christ revealed in water, bread, and wine is a breaker of barriers among people, a builder of community, a champion of the poor and marginalized, the Prince of Peace, and the advocate of justice. The living out of our identity as a people of the sacraments requires us to join with Christ in this work. The sacraments carry with them a moral imperative for holy living. The grace they offer is free but not cheap. Indeed, it is a grace that costs us our lives as expressed in Wesley's Covenant Prayer:

> I am no longer my own, but thine.
> Put me to what thou wilt, rank me with whom thou wilt.
> Put me to doing, put me to suffering.
> Let me be employed by thee or laid aside for thee,
> exalted for thee or brought low by thee.
> Let me be full, let me be empty.
> Let me have all things, let me have nothing.[7]

SUGGESTIONS FOR THE GROUP SESSION

Gather Supplies

Several copies of *The United Methodist Hymnal* and *The Faith We Sing*; Bibles; large sheets of paper or poster paper and pens; *By Water and the Spirit: A United Methodist Understanding of Baptism*; *This Holy Mystery: A United Methodist Understanding of Holy Communion*; *The Interpreter's Dictionary of the Bible*; *The United Methodist Book of Worship*; *The Book of Discipline of The United Methodist Church, 2004*; *The Book of Resolutions of The United Methodist Church, 2004*; and *The Oxford Dictionary of the Christian Church*.

Arrange the Learning Area

• Ahead of time, prepare a worship center. Find a small table. Cover it with an attractive tablecloth or a piece of fabric. Place a candle in a candleholder and the elements for Holy Communion on the worship center. Also place a pitcher of water and a bowl on the worship center. Light the candle.

• Make sure everyone has a place to sit. Arrange the learning area to facilitate group discussion.

Lead the Session

• Pray together for God's guidance as you explore issues and questions related to living as baptized and communing Christians.

• Read the opening paragraph and ask, "How should we live as baptized and communing Christians? What does "so what?" suggest to you? List responses on a large piece of paper.

• Read each of the sections in the chapter using the questions in the sections to stimulate discussion.

• Plan a service or a mission project for your group that will express what you have learned in this study of the sacraments.

• Sing or read the hymn "Now Let Us From This Table Rise" (Hymnal, 634).

• Close the session by inviting participants to view the worship center that has the elements of Holy Communion and baptism on it. Pray together by offering thanks to God for the gift of the church as a sacramental community and for all opportunities to serve Christ and one another through the church.

Notes

Notes to Chapter 1

1. *The United Methodist Hymnal*, 623.
2. From *Confessions*, by Augustine (Book 1, Chapter 1); *http://www.our ladyswarriors.org/saints/augcon1.htm#chap1*.
3. From *God the Invisible King*, Chapter 4, by H. G. Wells (1917); *http://www.online-literature.com/wellshg/invisibleking/*.
4. From *The Silver Chair*, by C. S. Lewis (Macmillan Books, 1953); pages 16-17.
5. From *The Works of John Wesley: The Bicentennial Edition*, Volume 1, Sermon 16, edited by Albert Cook Outler (Abingdon Press, 1984); page 381.
6. From "Article 7a: Baptism," by Brad Waggoner, in *Baptist Faith and Message* (August 21, 2002).
7. From *The Book of Discipline of The United Methodist Church, 2004* (Copyright © 2004 by The United Methodist Publishing House), ¶ 103; page 74.
8. For more information about the number of sacraments, see "Sacrament" in *The Oxford Dictionary of the Christian Church*; pages 1218-19.
9. From *The Book of Resolutions of The United Methodist Church, 2004* (Copyright © 2004 by The United Methodist Publishing House); pages 857-76.
10. From *The Book of Resolutions*; pages 883-931.
11. Study editions of these documents are available: *By Water and the Spirit: Making Connections for Identity and Ministry,* by Gayle Carlton Felton (Discipleship Resources, 1998) and *This Holy Mystery: A United Methodist Understanding of Holy Communion,* by Gayle Carlton Felton (Discipleship Resources, 2006).

Notes to Chapter 2

1. *Hymnal*, 605.
2. From *Remember Who You Are: Baptism, a Model for Christian Life,* by William H. Willimon (The Upper Room, 1980); pages 110-14.

Notes

3. From "A Treatise on Baptism," by John Wesley, in *The Works of John Wesley,* Volume 10, edited by Thomas Jackson.
4. *Hymnal,* 32-54.
5. From *By Water and the Spirit,* Study Edition, by Gayle Felton (Discipleship Resources, 1998); pages 1-6.
6. From *By Water and the Spirit,* Study Edition; pages 9-13, 17-18.
7. *Hymnal,* 33; emphasis added.
8. From *By Water and the Spirit,* Study Edition; pages 21-22, 27-32.
9. *Hymnal,* 33.
10. *Hymnal,* 34.
11. *Hymnal,* 34.
12. *Hymnal,* 34.
13. *Hymnal,* 34.
14. *Hymnal,* 34.
15. *Hymnal,* 34.
16. *Hymnal,* 35.
17. *Hymnal,* 35.
18. *Hymnal,* 35.
19. *Hymnal,* 36.
20. *Hymnal,* 36.
21. *Hymnal,* 36.
22. *Hymnal,* 37
23. *Hymnal,* 37.
24. From *By Water and the Spirit,* Study Edition; pages 17-24.
25. *Hymnal,* 37
26. *Hymnal,* 37.
27. *Hymnal,* 50-54.
28. From *By Water and the Spirit,* Study Edition; pages 35-40.
29. Today, some congregations receive requests from people who want to profess their faith and become members of the church of Jesus Christ but do not want to become members of The United Methodist Church. Currently the denomination has no provision in either church rules or rituals for this option.
30. *Hymnal,* 38.
31. *Hymnal,* 38.

Notes to Chapter 3

1. *The Faith We Sing,* 2248.
2. From *The Oxford Dictionary of the Christian Church* (Oxford Press, USA); pages 701-702.

Notes to Chapter 4

1. *Hymnal,* 616.
2. From *Three by Flannery O'Connor,* by Flannery O'Connor (Signet, 1964); pages 197-98.
3. From *Eating and Drinking at the Welcome Table: The Holy Supper for All People,* by William K. McElvaney (Chalice Press, 1998); pages 1, 14.
4. From *This Holy Mystery: A United Methodist Understanding of Holy Communion, Study Edition,* by Gail Carlton Felton (Discipleship Resources, 2006); pages 23-35.
5. From *The Works of John Wesley* (Outler); page 585.
6. From *This Holy Mystery,* Study Edition; pages 15-16.
7. From *The Works of John Wesley* (Outler); page 429.
8. From *The Works of John Wesley* (Outler); page 429.
9. *Hymnal,* 12.
10. *Hymnal,* 12.
11. *Hymnal,* 12.
12. From *This Holy Mystery,* Study Edition; page 35.
13. *Hymnal,* 12.
14. *Hymnal,* 12.
15. *Hymnal,* 12.
16. *Hymnal,* 12.
17. From Collect for Peace in the *Book of Common Prayer;* page 17.
18. *Hymnal,* 12.
19. *Hymnal,* 12.
20. *Hymnal,* 12.
21. *Hymnal,* 12.
22. *Hymnal,* 13.
23. *Hymnal,* 13.
24. From *This Holy Mystery,* Study Edition; pages 35-37.
25. *Hymnal,* 9.
26. *The United Methodist Book of Worship,* 54-80.
27. *Book of Worship,* 54.
28. *Book of Worship,* 54.
29. *Book of Worship,* 54.
30. *Book of Worship,* 54.
31. *Book of Worship,* 54.
32. *Book of Worship,* 54.
33. *Hymnal,* 9.
34. *Book of Worship,* 54.
35. *Hymnal,* 9.
36. *Hymnal,* 9.
37. *Hymnal,* 10.
38. *Hymnal,* 10.
39. *Hymnal,* 10.

40. *Hymnal*, 10.
41. *Hymnal*, 10.
42. *Hymnal*, 10.
43. *Hymnal*, 10.
44. *Hymnal*, 10.
45. *Hymnal*, 10.
46. *Hymnal*, 10.
47. *Hymnal*, 11.
48. *Hymnal*, 11.
49. From *This Holy Mystery*, Study Edition; pages 50-53.
50. *Hymnal*, 11.
51. *Hymnal*, 11.
52. *Hymnal*, 11.
53. *Hymnal*, 11.
54. From *This Holy Mystery*, Study Edition; pages 57-59.

Notes to Chapter 5

1. *Hymnal*, 627.
2. From *The Works of John Wesley* (Outler); pages 428-29.
3. From *This Holy Mystery*, Study Edition; page 34.
4. *Hymnal*, 43.
5. A resolution supporting use of "the pure unfermented juice of the vine" was passed by the 1996 General Conference, but it expired under the eight-year rule when it was not renewed in 2004. Hymnals and books of worship published during that period included the rubric.

Notes to Chapter 6

1. From *A Collection of Hymns for Public, Social, and Domestic Worship* (John Early, 1847).
2. *Hymnal*, 634.
3. *Hymnal*, 11.
4. From "Good News to the Poor: Baptism as Liberation," by Gail Carlton Felton, in *Quarterly Review: A Journal of Theological Resources for Ministry*, Volume 14, Number 4, Winter 1994; page 387.
5. From "Embodying the Justice of God: the Eucharist's Prophetic Power May Be a Well-kept Secret," by William K. Mcelvaney in *Zion's Herald*, September/October 2005; page 39.
6. *Book of Discipline*, ¶ 101; page 48.
7. *Hymnal*, 607.